TESTIMONIALS

Engaging style, easy to read, great mix of theory and live experience. Phillip Ralph has written a practical handbook for leaders who want to dig deeper, and transform themselves and their organisations. Courage required. Faint-hearted types advised to steer clear of this book.

Phil Clothier | Barrett Values Centre

Leadership Without Silver Bullets is a must read for anyone who seeks to be a successful leader in today's world in any capacity, whether in an organisation or the community. Phillip Ralph exposes some of the flaws in traditional leadership thinking and offers a fresh paradigm which calls us all to respond differently to the adaptive challenges we face. The book provides a practical model to use to develop leadership at all levels of an organisation.

John Fogarty | St John of God Health Care

I have had the privilege of seeing the results of Phillip Ralph's work as a leadership coach. He is outstanding. I can highly recommend this book as both practical and inspiring with valuable insights on how leadership in organisations really works.

Michael Rennie | McKinsey

This work exposes many of the myths about leadership and presents a very clear and practical guide to what *effective* leadership is really about. Any organisation would benefit by following the principles outlined to raise the bar on leadership and organisational performance.

Louis Hawke | Company Director & Equity Investor

A compelling, insightful and practical guide on leadership. Drawing on wisdom from historical figures, leadership experts and the author's personal experiences, it is a call to action for leadership in the 21st century. Phillip has done a great job of not only synthesising the latest in leadership theory but adding new and practical insights that will assist anyone who is passionate about their own leadership journey or making a difference in their places of work.

Mark Priede | Bendelta

Phillip has done a fine job in debunking the modern myths on leadership, whilst constructing an accessible and eminently applicable model for today's organisational challenges. He demonstrates that leadership is shared and fluid, and the best leaders are those who enable others to lead, at any level of the organisation. I recommend this work to any who want to see real change and growth in themselves and their organisation.

Greg Camm | Company Director

This is not just another book claiming to deliver the secrets of leadership success. Instead, through the use of thought-provoking examples and practical ideas, Phillip shares his unique take on what defines real leaders. The Seven Spheres of Leadership Mastery Model will clearly assist organisations and HR professionals by providing a platform and language for discussing leadership capability. It certainly has influenced the way in which I think about what makes a great leader.

Shaneen Argall | Arnold Bloch Leibler

Phil has an amazing ability to quickly and succinctly help the reader get to grips with the world of leadership development, its history and its challenges. Phil has nailed it in his Leadership Declaration. This insight helps us understand that effective leadership is not just in the hands of a chosen few but rather we are all leaders in our own rights and can make a difference in our communities and businesses by applying a few simple but powerful techniques. Most importantly, it expresses the need for true leaders to be values-driven and to have the courage to do things differently. Underpinning his thinking are years of practical leadership development experience, robust models and the use of pragmatic examples that every leader can relate to.

Anthony Youds | LeaderFit

Leadership Without Silver Bullets is an informative read for anyone who leads a team and is seeking guidance on how to achieve employee engagement. Through personal experiences and straightforward analysis of recent leadership studies, this book reminds the reader of the modelling from school days to boardroom, which has led to the dominance of uninspiring, individualist, command-and-control management styles. This thought-provoking book may well be the catalyst for readers to develop a shared leadership approach to allow their disempowered teams to flourish.

Erin Duncan | Victoria Police

As the CEO of a children's charity determined to create a better world for children experiencing disadvantage, I believe investment in our people is paramount. When our work is about making sure that vulnerable children have what they need but resources are limited, it is imperative that we actively unleash our collective capacity and wisdom to make a difference. *Leadership Without Silver Bullets* is an accessible read that inspires reflection and determination to be the kind of leader who not only brings out the best in everyone, but enables the change that we want to see in the world.

Mandy Burns | Director

This book highlights and identifies some new and at times challenging thoughts on leadership, which will have a positive impact on all who are courageous enough to not only read the book but implement some personal and team changes. Phil has drawn upon his deep experience in working in many different management and leadership roles during his working life. The stated aim of the book 'To inspire and ignite leadership action that makes a difference for you, your organisation and the world' particularly resonated. I believe current and aspiring leaders and managers should put this on their must-read list.

Peter Callaway | WorkSafe Australia

LEADERSHIP

without

SILVER BULLETS

LEADERSHIP
without
SILVER BULLETS

A guide to accelerating
team performance

PHILLIP RALPH

© 2017 Phillip Ralph
First published in 2010 by The Leadership Sphere Pty Ltd | Melbourne
Revised edition printed in 2017 by Baker Street Press | Melbourne
ISBN 9780994321466

National Library of Australia Cataloguing-in-Publication entry.
Creator: Ralph, Phillip, author.

Title:	Leadership without silver bullets: a guide to accelerating team performance / Phillip Ralph.
Editor:	Joanna Yardley.
Edition:	Revised edition.
ISBN:	9780994321466 (paperback)
Notes:	Includes bibliographical references.
Subjects:	Leadership.
	Self-actualization (Psychology)
	Creative ability in business.
	Career development.

Other Creators/Contributors: Yardley, Joanna, editor.

Every effort has been made to trace (and seek permission for use of) the original source of material used within this book. Where the attempt has been unsuccessful, the publisher would be pleased to hear from the author/publisher to rectify any omission.

To those who have the courage to lead and
make a positive difference.

CONTENTS

Preface ix

Part 1: Leadership Today and Why It's Not Working

1: Follow the Leader 5

2: Leadership and the Elite...11

3: Theories That Have Driven Leadership Thinking....................... 17

Part 2: Why Most Leaders Don't Lead

4: The Industrial Age Leadership Paradigm.................................... 25

5: The Age of Passivity 31

6: Counterfeit Leadership.. 39

7: The Delusion of Solutions..43

Part 3: A Leadership Declaration – Our Vision for the Future

8: A Leadership Declaration – Our Vision for the Future of
Leadership 53

Part 4: The Seven Spheres of Leadership Mastery

9: The Seven Spheres of Leadership Mastery 77

10: Leadership in Practice 89

11: Influencing without Authority 97

Part 5: The Seven Spheres of Leadership Mastery in Practice

12: Manage and Lead Change...109

13: Action-Oriented 113

14: Synergy 117

15: Truth 123

16: Engage...129

17: Resilience..137

18: You 143

19: Final Thoughts...147

About the Author 151

Contact/Organisation Details..153

References 157

Bibliography 161

On-line Resources..164

PREFACE

It has been six years since the first edition of Leadership Without Silver Bullets was published. Many people—whether relatively new to leadership or with decades of management experience—have provided feedback that the book challenged many of their fundamental beliefs about what it means to be a leader in an organisational or community context. And that's exactly why I wrote this book in the first place. For too long we have endured rehashed, stale theories on a subject that, let's face it, has been done to death.

We hear and read about leadership in popular press, traditional media, social media, schools, sporting clubs and politics. So it may be a bold claim when I say that this book will help you think about leadership in a very different way, and that there is a very good chance you will actually be a different leader as a result. But after six years and several thousand people having read the first edition, I can say with some confidence that this is in fact true for many who take the time to read the book in its entirety.

A cautionary note if I may: unlike many authors who offer the seductive claim that you can pick up their respective books, turn to any page and start reading, I don't recommend this approach. It unfortunately mirrors how we generally treat the subject of leadership: in short, spasmodic bursts of attention and enthusiasm that usually dissipate over time.

The journey to becoming a better leader is too important and too complex to treat in a fleeting or superficial way. I recommend you fight against a world that rewards and reinforces short-termism, quick-fixes and tidbits, by reading this book in solid blocks of time (which work for you). Only then will you get the most from the story that is layered throughout the book supported by data, research and evidence.

So, after six years, where are we at?

In some ways nothing has changed, and in other ways a lot has changed.

What hasn't changed?

- The relentless pressure on organisations and managers to deliver results.
- Whether corporations succeed or fail, we somehow usually end up talking about the leader and his or her leadership.
- A focus on improving the quality of leadership through developing people.
- Organisations trying to 'crack the code' of great leadership development.
- The fundamentals of leadership remain largely the same.

What *has* changed?

- With globalisation, technological innovation and the connectedness of people, the pace of change has become even faster.
- The importance of leadership has become even more central to the success of organisations.
- The ability to adopt a leadership style centered on influence rather the power granted by a formal role or position is even more important.

Why leadership matters today more than ever

The Centre for Workplace Leadership at Melbourne University undertook the Study of Australian Leadership (SAL) during

2016, which re-validated what we have known for some time. It concluded that leadership and management matter for workplace performance by driving the development of core organisational capabilities associated with meeting and exceeding targets, and performance relative to competitors and profitability. It also reported that investment in leadership capability pays in many ways, including leader self-efficacy (I believe I *can* lead) and leadership capabilities, which, in turn, are associated with better performance and more innovation.

What is the current state of leadership and management in Australia?

The same SAL report, however, paints a bleak picture of leadership and management capability in Australia including:

- Many Australian workplaces are underperforming.
- Many Australian organisations do not get the basics right.
- Few Australian organisations report high levels of innovation.
- Many Australian leaders are not well trained for the job.
- Too many Australian organisations underinvest in leadership development, especially at the frontline.
- Leadership in Australian organisations does not reflect wider social diversity.
- Many senior leaders do not draw on strategic advice in making decisions about the future.

The report provides a sobering reminder to organisations and people like me, who work in the business of developing leaders that we have a long way to go. Together, we need to work harder to deepen our understanding of what effective leadership is in today's changing context, and identify the best approach and methodology mix for that context.

As I wrote in my first edition, the words 'leadership' and 'leader' are often used whether or not real leadership is present. We often assign a role rather than an action to the word 'leader'. Despite this, there remains a crisis of leadership identity. Am I a leader? What does that really mean, anyway? For example, I've asked hundreds of groups (mostly executives and senior managers) what they think leadership means. I get almost as many answers as there are people in the room. I am also dismayed by the largely wasted expenditure on misguided leadership development. Sadly, leadership is perhaps the most overused and abused word in modern organisational language.

While this book is not about trying to settle the leadership score once and for all, it does aim to provide a fresh and useful perspective, whether you are a member of a board, a chief executive, executive, middle manager, HR professional, or someone who chooses to make a difference. While I would not claim to have invented a new paradigm (another overused word), my hope and intention is that my small contribution, in this book and ongoing work, builds on the emerging new paradigm in a meaningful way.

How this book is structured

In Part 1: Leadership Today and Why It's Not Working, I share some things that I and others have learnt trying to understand and navigate the often messy territory of leadership, while drawing on my 20+ years working with thousands of leaders in dozens of industries and roles. In Part 2: Why Most Leaders Don't Lead, I present an argument on why I think we do not lead effectively, and make the case that effective leadership is more important than ever before. In Part 3: A Leadership Declaration – Our Vision for the Future, I present a fresh approach to leadership—one that provides clarity and focus on where and how we need to develop leadership capability, irrespective of role or title. I also present a refreshed leadership model that now draws more attention to influencing without authority, managing complexity and leading change. (This edition has two additional chapters covering these important topics.)

Finally, in Parts 4 and 5: The Seven Spheres of Leadership Mastery, I bring our Leadership Declaration to life through a rolling case study and real-life examples. During this process, my hope is that you will take the opportunity to reflect on your own leadership and how it relates to who you are, your work and the world around you.

My vision for our organisations, communities and indeed, you, hasn't changed, in that I hope by reading this book you will become clearer about the type of leadership you need and want in your own organisation, and that your own leadership journey is enriched in a tangible way.

Phillip Ralph

ACKNOWLEDGEMENTS

This book has really been written over the last two-and-half decades. It is the product of many experiences in many different contexts. During that time, learning and curiosity have been two core drivers of mine. Friends and family still wonder how I can read leadership literature in my down time. My thirst for knowledge and understanding of leadership, team development and culture change continues unabated.

I have worked with many truly amazing leaders, both as part of an organisation and in a leadership consulting capacity. These men and women have inspired me to enhance my own leadership capability and to stretch myself in the work I perform with clients. The trust that clients place in me and my colleagues at The Leadership Sphere in supporting them to achieve breakthrough performance continues to be a humbling experience. I have also worked with many people I feel proud to call colleagues, many of whom are my best friends and confidants. I thank you from the bottom of my heart for your support, growth and friendship.

I would especially like to thank my wife, Kerrie, and children, Thomas, Emma, and Caitlin, for your love and support.

PART 1:

LEADERSHIP
TODAY AND WHY
IT'S NOT WORKING

CHAPTER 1

FOLLOW THE LEADER

The greatest obstacle to discovery is not
ignorance – it is the illusion of knowledge.
—Daniel J. Boorstin

At a very early age, I learned that the leader was the person in front of the group, showing everyone what they needed to do and where they needed to go. Like many young children, I was taught a game at primary school called follow-the-leader. I dare say you were taught this exact same game, or perhaps a slight variation (does *Simon says* ring a bell?). The game basically entailed a designated leader positioned out the front giving orders and demonstrating to others the required path and actions. The followers (in this case a group of rowdy five-year-olds) were meant to do and say exactly what the leader told us to do and say. If you didn't comply, the consequences were severe and swift, accompanied by cries of *you're out*!

During my formative years, and later when I entered the workforce, I have continued to receive many messages about leadership. 'Leader' and 'leadership' were terms used in many different ways and contexts like sport, politics, at home, community groups, the military and, of course, in organisations.

As a keen entrant to the workforce, I soon noticed that those in positions of formal authority (usually managers in charge of other people and resources) were bestowed the title of leader, usually when they managed the people and resources as expected. These same people were called excellent leaders if they were able to co-ordinate and control people and resources better than others could.

For example, early in my career, I was seconded to a government department to write a report on whether illicit drugs should be legalised. I worked under an executive-level manager who was responsible for many smart professional people, yet he ran the department like a school. He had devised a myriad of rigid managerial controls and supervisory tasks to make sure 'no one stepped out of line'. Even though the climate was devoid of energy and enthusiasm, he was touted as a key leader because he (apparently) managed the department well, with everyone simply following him. I was very pleased to leave six months later when the report was finalised.

There were also heavy expectations on leaders to know more than everyone else, particularly the technical aspects of their job. And, ipso facto, they were expected to possess more answers to the problems faced in organisations. Again, managers who seemed to have more answers than others were rewarded, usually by being called a leader.

This made perfect sense to me. Isn't that why leaders are paid more, I thought? Not much has changed today. In my work as a coach I am privileged to hear the stories of hundreds of people across many industries. One of the most common conversations is how to let go of the 'reins of control' so that others may grow and develop. We seem to hold on to the belief that leaders must somehow control everything.

A Simple Test

When working with leaders, I ask them to perform a simple test. First, I ask them to draw a person—representing a direct report. Then I ask them to draw a box around that person to represent the amount of 'space' or autonomy they think they give that person. At this point, they usually draw something that looks like the first box below (The Fantasy). In their minds, they believe they create an environment where people feel empowered to be their best.

'A': The Fantasy

'B': The Reality

Figure 1: Managers versus team members' perception of autonomy

Then I ask their direct reports to draw the same figure and box representing how much autonomy they actually get from their leader. The resulting box is usually much smaller and looks more like The Reality. They feel constrained and directed – far from an empowered individual who is at their best.

In a workshop context, I will ask a group, 'How big should I draw the box when you think about your team and leadership style?' It usually looks like box A. Then I ask them to think about their own manager and the amount of autonomy they get from him or her— it usually looks like box B.

I have also tried this experiment with 100+ people in the room, by asking each person to rate their own leadership capability and the capability of the group (the other 99 people sitting in the room).

Using instant online polling, the results are both amusing and challenging. Almost without exception, people rate themselves higher than their peers by as much as 30 per cent.

While I understand that this isn't a well-constructed, randomised double-blind study, it does highlight an interesting phenomenon that can keep us stuck. It's why, for example, 80 per cent of drivers think they're better than average – a statistical impossibility! Most people *overestimate* their own positive attributes or behavioural standards, and *overstate* the negative attributes and behaviours of those around them. This can then create a cycle which may not accurately represent actual development needs. The figure below shows how this can become a cycle of complacency.

Figure 2: Cycle of complacency

Politics, People and the Pros

My beliefs and views about leadership continue to be influenced by the people and events around me today, as well as from people and events in history.

Winston Churchill, known mainly for his speeches and leadership during World War II, was referred to as a great leader despite being voted out of government as soon as the war was over (Prince, et al., 2002). In the military, people such as Alexander the Great, known for his tactical ability, his conquests, and for spreading Greek civilisation into the East, were also touted as leaders. Leadership, from this perspective, was about taking charge, exercising the full force of one's authority and winning at all costs.

I later learned about Mohandas Karamchand Gandhi (better known as Mahatma Gandhi), the pre-eminent political and spiritual leader of India during the Indian independence movement. Gandhi inspired civil rights movements and freedom across the globe. Leadership through this lens was about influencing others to make a positive difference in the world.

Then there were the iconic sporting heroes I idolised as a child ('the pros'). These were the men and women who achieved amazing athletic feats and were admired for their leadership qualities. Locally, there was Sir Donald Bradman, whose cricketing prowess and gentlemanly character were unsurpassed. In basketball, Michael Jordan had the ball on a string, and knew ahead of time what was going to happen on the court. Within their own sports, they were called heroes and leaders. For me, leadership in the sporting arena is about fulfilling one's potential, pushing the limits of what is thought possible, and above all, conquering the competition and surpassing one's own self-imposed limits.

Summary

Despite 'leader' being used in so many different contexts, I thought I knew what effective leadership meant, and what I needed to do to be called a leader.

Our beliefs about leadership and followership are shaped from a very early age through playing games, and the messages we receive. The terms leader and leadership mean different things depending on the context; for example, in sport, politics, at home, community groups, the military and, of course, in organisations.

Traditional Domains of Leadership

1. Politics   (taking charge, exercising authority, winning)

2. Military   (rank, conquests, heroism)

3. Influencing others (to make a difference)

4. Sport   (fulfilling our potential, pushing the limits, winning)

In an organisation, those who hold a position of formal authority are referred to as leaders, and those without formal authority are not. The leaders are expected to have the answers to organisational problems and challenges and provide these nuggets of brilliance and insight to non-leaders.

The very nature and purpose of leadership varies according to the lens through which we observe it; despite the myriad of ways to view leadership, some may believe they have a good understanding of it.

CHAPTER 2

LEADERSHIP AND THE ELITE

*We learn more by looking for the answer to a question and
not finding it than we do from learning the answer itself.*
—Lloyd Alexander

Leadership Confusion

As a result of my early experiences, I learned that our view of what it means to be a leader is shaped from the time we begin to learn the alphabet. I also learned (at least in my mind) that leadership was largely inaccessible to the masses. Therefore, as a young adult I had the mindset that to be a leader I needed to be one of four types of person:

• An heroic leader on the battlefield.

• Someone who holds high public office (or similar).

• An elite sportsperson.

• A senior person in an organisation.

I also suspect many others learned early on that real leadership was unattainable. I am constantly surprised by how few hands are raised when I ask the following question of a group or team: How many of you in this room consider yourselves to be leaders? You can almost smell the deprecating self-analysis!

In fact, our beliefs about leadership are shaped by so many different people, sources and contexts that it's almost incomprehensible.

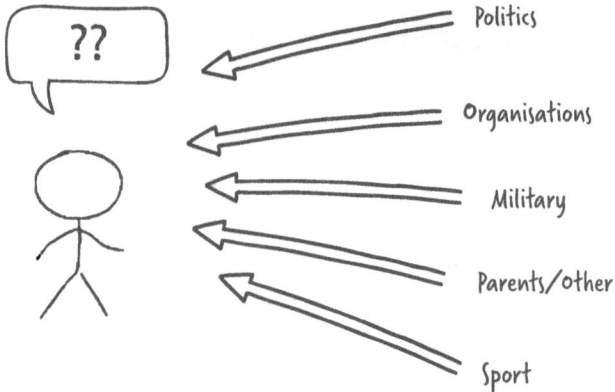

Figure 3: Multiple messages we receive about leadership

Is it any wonder that we are confused about what leadership actually is, and whether we are worthy enough to call ourselves a leader?

Over time, however, I came to the realisation that my view of leadership was overly simplistic. As is the case with many domains of life, and frustratingly so, the more I learned about leadership, the more I realised what I didn't know. As a result, I became hugely invested in trying to work out what made people tick. I was especially interested in leadership and the dynamics that existed within teams, particularly given their critical nature to the success of most organisations.

The Seduction of Having the Answers

I have pondered many questions. What does real leadership look like? What qualities or attributes were needed to be an effective leader? Why some people are called leaders and others are not?

What is the difference between managers and leaders? Why are some people successful in life while others, with apparently equal talent and motivation, are left to languish? Why, in organisations, are some people able to inspire others while others are loathed?

Perhaps coincidentally, or because of my fascination in understanding human potential in the context of leadership, I was called upon more and more to help organisations develop their leadership capability and team performance.

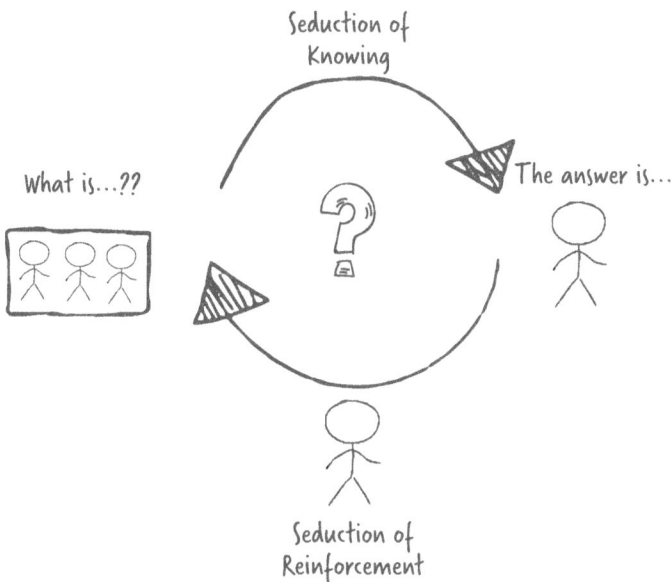

Figure 4: The seduction of knowing the answer

As I moved into different positions and roles, a theme emerged. Others looked to me not just for guidance around leadership and team performance, but for the answers to many of the big leadership questions previously mentioned. The more people asked, the more I felt compelled to give them the answers, so I happily (and naively) provided what I thought at the time was the answer. I was seduced by the lure of having to 'know it all'.

Paradoxically, the dilemmas I had observed other leaders wrestle with while finding the answers to a myriad of organisational problems was now happening to me – I just couldn't see it.

As I became more entrenched in leadership, team development and culture change programs, I began to reflect on my deepest beliefs about leadership and people. Were people just resources to be managed and controlled? Could sound management and effective leadership coexist within the one person? With its emphasis on leadership, followership and control, was our whole management and leadership paradigm flawed?

I thought more about Churchill's speeches. While, at the time, they were clearly of world importance, they seemed a million miles from my own life and reality. I further examined my limited beliefs about who could exercise leadership, and under what circumstances. I also began to understand that while managers and leaders can be the same, few managers actually led effectively.

In my view, there was very little correlation between a person's job title and what they actually did. Some of the most junior people I met displayed real leadership, while those in senior positions and with years of experience often failed to lead effectively. Many had become frozen by their own fears, expending unnecessary energy trying to maintain their status and ego while political game-playing.

I was hired to work in a major financial institution that was collectively responsible for the implementation and integration of major systems worth several billion dollars. The team was so inwardly focused, I was amazed it achieved much at all. Team members were putting a lot of energy and focus on protecting their own turf, one-upmanship, and destructive side conversations to undermine each other ensuring the status quo was largely maintained. The head of the team insisted on establishing punishing deadlines, which created (or at least contributed to) serious personal problems such as relationship breakdowns and poor health.

Experiences like these created fire in my belly as I worked to understand why some perfectly rational, intelligent people acted in a perfectly irrational and very unintelligent way, and why so many people in those situations failed to lead effectively.

And so continued my quest, over twenty years, to identify 'the answer'.

Summary

What we learn about leadership from a young age can make it look like it's inaccessible to the masses (i.e. if you're not a military hero; do not hold a senior public office or organisational position; or are not an elite athlete).

Our notions of what it means to be a leader can constrain our identity and self-belief about our leadership capabilities.

Given our understanding of leadership, it is easy to be seduced into giving people what we see as 'the answer'.

Job titles bear little resemblance to people's effectiveness as leaders.

When smart people come together in a team, they usually do really dumb things, largely born out of a need for self-protection.

serious personal problems such as relationship breakdowns and poor health.

CHAPTER 3

THEORIES THAT HAVE DRIVEN LEADERSHIP THINKING

It is the theory that decides what can be observed.
—Albert Einstein

Leadership Theories

Along the way, I've wrestled with this notion of leadership. My views and beliefs have morphed over time, almost running in parallel with leadership trends and theories at the time. While early leadership theories focused on the qualities that distinguished leaders from followers, subsequent theories looked at other variables, such as situational factors and skill levels (Drinon, n.d.).

Let's examine the main theories or paradigms that have shaped many of the programs and development activities in organisations.

Great Man theories assume that the capacity for leadership is inherent—that great leaders are born, not made. These theories often portray great leaders as heroic, mythic, and destined to rise to leadership when needed, for example, Alexander the Great and Winston Churchill. We see this paradigm played out almost weekly in the financial and popular press where an all-conquering CEO is featured on the cover.

In some ways, *Trait* theories are similar to *Great Man* theories, in that they assume that people inherit certain qualities and traits that make them better suited to leadership. Trait theories often identify particular personality or behavioural characteristics shared by leaders. Both theories have shortcomings. For example, when people possess the requisite traits or 'stuff' but fail to lead, or conversely, where people have demonstrated leadership, yet may lack many of the 'must haves' these theories demand. In my view, the belief that effective leaders have a shopping list of traits or competencies can hold people back from stepping into the action of leading, as they recognise a gap between themselves and the 'ideal leader'.

Contingency theories of leadership focus on particular variables related to the environment that might determine which particular style of leadership is best suited to the situation. According to this theory, no leadership style is best in all situations. Unfortunately, many leaders justify destructive, aggressive and toxic behaviours based on the false belief (or rationalisation) that 'it was what was needed at the time'.

Situational theories propose that leaders should choose the best course of action based on the situation. Different styles of leadership may be more appropriate for certain types of decision-making. While the premise is sound, I often wonder how people achieve this in reality. How do I know what style of leadership is needed for this situation?

Behavioural theories of leadership are based on the belief that great leaders are made, not born. People can learn to become leaders through teaching and observation. The dangers observed with this theory are similar to *Great Man* and *Trait* theories, in that the ever-increasing long list of behaviours often espoused as prerequisites to lead effectively, are often unrealistic and don't take into account human frailties and the different contexts in which leaders operate.

Participative theories of leadership dictate that leaders take into account the views of others before making decisions. Again, this is fine if you know where, when and how to do this. I've seen many leaders ricochet from being overly democratic and consultative, to authoritative and demanding.

Management theories of leadership (also known as *Transactional* theories) focus on the role of supervision, organisation and group performance, and are largely based on a system of reward and punishment. These theories tend to reinforce the archaic notion born in the industrial age that we need to closely manage and control people. The truth is that we need to manage and control *things,* and lead and empower people. Today, we tend to over-manage and under-lead.

Finally, *Relationship* theories (also known as *Transformational* theories) focus on the connections formed between leaders and followers. In this theory, leaders motivate and inspire people to see the purpose behind the task, as well as wanting each person to fulfil his or her potential. Relationship theories stand up well under scrutiny, providing leaders with the know-how to effectively balance a focus on 'relationship' with 'task'. These activities go hand-in-hand, and should not be approached separately, for example, *Let's get the job done first and we'll look after the team dynamics and relationship stuff later.* The team dynamics and relationship stuff are often left dormant and unattended until the annual executive retreat at a five-star resort. Wrong!

While all of these theories contribute to the body of knowledge and the practice of leadership, they each are not sufficient on their own, and have created a lot of confusion in people's minds about how to proceed, either in developing leadership capability or in what it means to lead.

The Big Secret about Leadership

So after a 20-year quest, what is the big secret I've discovered about leadership? Well ... the big secret is that there is no big secret. Despite what hundreds, if not thousands, of management books, articles and so-called experts tell you, there are no silver bullets. Perhaps your own experience has led you to the same conclusion.

However, if you are reading this book in the hope that there are some relatively simple ways to think about and practice leadership that are effective and within reach, then I have good news—there are.

There is no doubt that leadership can be a demanding activity. I am not trying to trivialise the challenges of leadership, because those challenges are very real. In my mind, *real* leadership means:

- Setting the aspiration or direction.
- Creating an environment where people thrive.
- Taking courageous action.
- Treading where others fear to tread.
- Challenging the status quo.
- Naming the 'elephants in the room'.
- Confronting poor behaviour or performance.
- Creating an environment of trust and respect for one another.
- Ensuring that solutions are well thought out and systemic, where appropriate.

There are a number of relatively simple things anyone can do to be a more effective leader – whether you are a CEO, divisional head, a manager of people, technical specialist, new manager or a community leader. Effective leadership ought not to be confined to particular roles or industries, either. Effective leadership is effective leadership, no matter where it occurs.

Summary

There are a number of leadership theories that endeavour to explain and understand leadership:

Great Man theories assume that the capacity for leadership is inherent— that great leaders are born, not made.

Trait theories also assume that people inherit certain qualities and traits that make them better suited to leadership.

Contingency theories focus on particular variables related to the environment that might determine which particular style of leadership is best suited to the situation.

Situational theories propose that leaders should choose the best course of action based on the situation.

Behavioural theories of leadership are based on the belief that great leaders are made, not born.

Participative theories of leadership dictate that leaders take into account the views of others before making decisions.

Management theories of leadership focus on the role of supervision, organisation and group performance, and are largely based on a system of reward and punishment.

Relationship theories focus on the connections formed between leaders and followers.

What is the 'big secret' of leadership? There are no silver bullets.

Real leadership means setting the aspiration, creating an environment where people thrive, thinking systemically, and taking courageous action.

PART 2:

WHY MOST LEADERS DON'T LEAD

CHAPTER 4

THE INDUSTRIAL AGE
LEADERSHIP PARADIGM

All our knowledge has its origins in our perceptions.
—Leonardo da Vinci

The Dominant Paradigm

We are currently locked in a dominant paradigm founded in the industrial age, where organisations were machines and people were things to be controlled. People were necessary but replaceable. This paradigm, while useful for the production of goods in a low or no-technology environment, is woefully inadequate for the 21st century.

According to Stephen Covey, many of our modern management practices come from the industrial age (Schein, 2006). These include:

- The belief that you control and manage people.
- The view of accounting that makes people an expense and machines assets – think about it.
- A carrot and stick motivational philosophy (rewards versus fear and punishment).

- Centralised budgeting where hierarchies and bureaucracies are formed to drive 'getting the numbers' – an obsolete reactive process.

The management of people as things, by those in authoritative positions, prevents others from tapping into their highest motivations, talents and potential. And the question that needs to be asked is: 'At what cost?'

Author John Gardner once said, 'Most ailing organisations have developed a functional blindness to their own defects.' (Gardner, 1965)

One of the most fascinating dissertations on leadership and the industrial age is by Joseph Rost (Rost, 1993), who says the industrial age paradigm of leadership is characterised by (among other things):

- A personalistic focus, since only great leaders do leadership.
- A promotion of an individualistic and self-interested outlook on life.
- An acceptance of a male model of behaviour and power (which has been labelled a leadership style).

Leadership and the 100-Year-Old Paradigm

Rost was intrigued with the idea that there must be a unifying theme or an holistic framework that made sense of 80–90 years of research and writing on the subject of leadership. The single paradigm he managed to find was the industrial paradigm—a distinctly individualistic framework. The second thing he discovered was that the basic ideas of leadership haven't changed much in 100 years. The same ideas have been recycled decade after decade in mainstream literature, and have not impacted on the accumulated wisdom of leadership (Rost, 1997).

Leaders and Followers ...

Rost also found that we believe the leader to be the one who 'does' leadership to others. This conclusion translates into the practice of thinking and acting as if the followers don't have anything to do with leadership. In fact, we have created a new word in the industrial paradigm to explain what followers do – they do followership. And the essence of being a follower is to be passive, submissive, subordinate, controlled, and directed.

Dee Hock, founder and CEO Emeritus of both Visa USA and Visa International, and author of *Birth of the Chaordic Age* believes that anyone who is coerced to the purposes, objectives, or preferences of another is not a follower in any true sense of the word, but an object of manipulation.

Examples of the leader-follower belief system are rife in organisations today. Much of the frustration expressed to me when coaching CEOs and executives is that they just can't seem to get people to 'comply' or do what they think should be done. In this scenario, many then externalise the problem by saying that they have motivation issues, or lack the skills to do the job.

I worked with an executive who believed that because he was the leader, others needed to just implement his plan to be successful. His style was aggressive, individualistic and highly ego-driven. He was right to some extent, because his area did deliver results but the costs were high. Many of his senior leaders hated working at the organisation, and others left. He was also having difficulty attracting talent into the business unit. When I dug a bit deeper, he confessed that he actually didn't want to live or lead this way. After a six-month coaching program, his beliefs about himself and others had transformed considerably, and his way of managing and leading shifted significantly. He moved to practising shared leadership and was reaping the benefits.

After years of researching leadership, which included 221 definitions of leadership in over 500 books and articles, Rost was led 'to the ultimate synthesis of the leadership literature', and boiled it down to two words: good management. Hence, there is no such thing as bad leadership because when leadership is bad it is characterised as just 'plain management'.

Good management means *effective* management that is above average, goes beyond expectations or promotes excellence. The leadership literature has denigrated management throughout the 20th century, insisting that we should understand leadership as superior to management—almost as if we don't need management.

Nothing could be further from the truth. So, almost without exception, the sole leader is touted as the person who 'does leadership' by creating a vision, taking charge and motivating others to follow. The current paradigm has created a leadership vacuum, where managers try to come up with the answers for everyone else to go away and implement. The 'I think, you do' phenomenon is alive and well.

Summary

Despite significant effort and attention, organisations are still largely locked into a dominant paradigm from the industrial age.

The dominant management paradigm prevents people from tapping into their highest motivations, talents and potential.

The basic ideas of leadership haven't changed much in 100 years, with many simply being recycled or repackaged.

The risk of the leader-follower model is that people become *passive, submissive, subordinate, controlled,* and *directed.*

The leadership literature has *denigrated management throughout* the 20th century, so leadership authors have insisted that we must understand leadership as *better than management.*

The current paradigm has created a *leadership vacuum,* where managers try to come up with the answers for everyone else to go away and implement.

CHAPTER 5

THE AGE OF PASSIVITY

*The smart way to keep people passive and obedient is
to strictly limit the spectrum of acceptable opinion, but
allow very lively debate within that spectrum...*
—Noam Chomsky

That's Not My Job

With the backdrop of global and organisational challenges firmly established, the role of organisations and their leaders in society is more critical than ever. Perhaps for the first time in history, leaders are under intense scrutiny. We are stuck, however, in what I call the Age of Passivity, where we practise 'follow the leader' and look to others to solve our problems rather than act powerfully within our spheres of influence.

Follow the Leader is still Pervasive

The Age of Passivity is symbolised by examples such as:

- People blaming others when things go wrong.
- Not taking responsibility.
- Not being accountable for results.
- Waiting for others to act before acting.
- Not making timely and effective decisions.
- Only acting in the interests of oneself or one's own team or silo.

In general, we rely too heavily on others to solve our problems—whether they are global issues or those that confront us daily at work.

For example, I recently walked into a reception area to see a health professional. The woman on the desk was well-groomed, middle-aged, appeared to be well educated, and was courteous and helpful. While talking, I couldn't help but notice the flickering light above us and said to the woman, "That must be really irritating!" She nodded, "Yes, it's been that way for weeks. But it's not my job to change it or get it fixed, so I guess it stays like that", she replied.

Her reply surprised me as much as it didn't. Inflexibility and the 'it's not my job' phenomenon permeates organisations. It may be more subtle than people saying the words aloud, but I would be surprised if you couldn't think of a few examples in your own organisation. The problem is we become blind, numb or both to it, so we fail to see it for what it is and take action accordingly. It happens with flickering lights, in teams, and across functions and divisions. If we tune in to it, we can see generous amounts of blame, denial, justification and a lack of accountability occurring every day of the week. Outcomes include cost blowouts, missed deadlines, frustrated and disengaged employees, and a negative impact on customer service. In essence, performance is severely impacted.

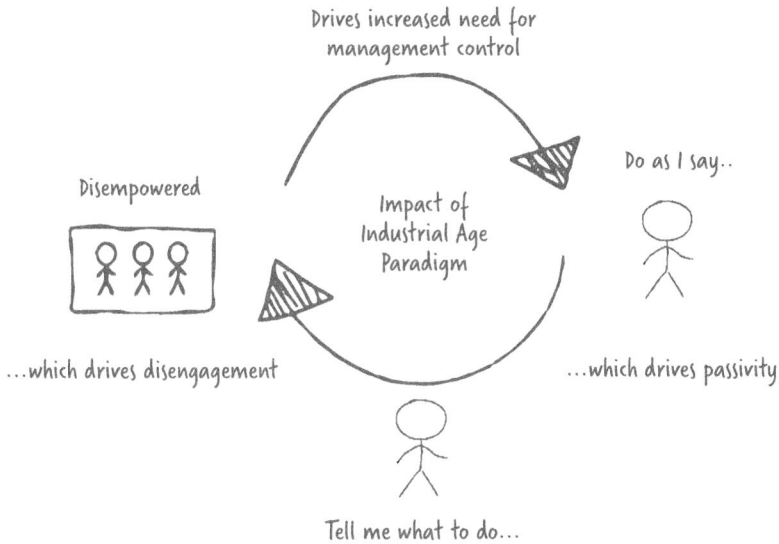

Drives increased need for
management control

Do as I say..

Disempowered

Impact of
Industrial Age
Paradigm

...which drives disengagement

...which drives passivity

Tell me what to do...

Figure 5: Impact of the industrial age paradigm on employees

The 'Fix It' Mentality

So, in the Age of Passivity, we tend to rely too heavily on others, particularly those in positions of authority or government, to fix things or to act first. Charles Handy, the futurist, wrote, 'We can't rely on governments to lead us. In democracies, governments have to go with the grain of public opinion or they won't get re-elected' (Handy, 2006). How many metaphorical flickering lights and receptionists do you have in your organisation? And more importantly, how much is it costing you?

The fact is that when it comes to solving our toughest challenges, no government, statutory body, CEO or any other individual can solve these problems in isolation, despite our apparent worship of the heroic CEO who will 'save' the organisation.

What's the problem with leaders providing solutions? When we over-rely on others for the answers, we contribute to a culture of passivity. This statement does not discount the role of those with technical expertise, because it is often appropriate, perhaps even necessary, to look to those with authoritative expertise to provide advice and counsel. But problems may occur in that scenario as well.

Figure 6: Tension between expectations and ability to create change

Let's assume John attends his family doctor with a suspected heart condition. John doesn't expect his doctor to say, 'Work it out for yourself.' In this situation, we expect to be given the answer and this is appropriate when the problem is a clear-cut technical problem with a clear-cut, known, tried-and-tested solution. In effect, we vest authority in the doctor in exchange for a service. For argument sake, let's say that after consulting his doctor and being referred to a specialist, John needs a bypass operation.

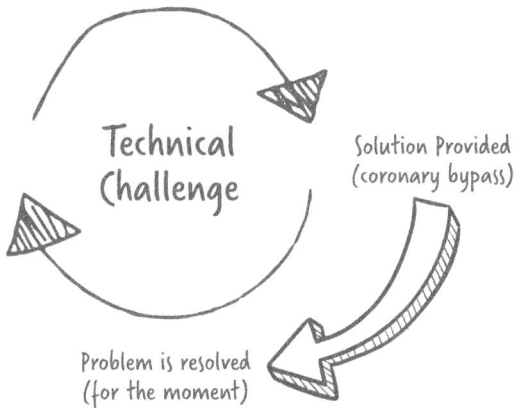

Technical Challenge

Solution Provided (coronary bypass)

Problem is resolved (for the moment)

Figure 7: Technical solutions work well for technical challenges

The surgeon performs the operation but John fails to make any lifestyle changes. In ten years his heart needs another overhaul. This is an act of passivity and a lack of responsibility – both from the patient and the surgeon. Both have failed to address the underlying issues of poor eating habits and a sedentary lifestyle. John has effectively deferred responsibility and accountability for managing his own health, without addressing the root causes.

This isn't particularly new or breakthrough thinking. We all know the old adage 'prevention is better than cure', or have heard the advice to avoid Band-Aid approaches, but we still fail to act appropriately. We know in real life, for example, that about 90 per cent of patients do not change their lifestyle after receiving a life-saving bypass operation (Deutschman, 2007). The fact remains that if organisations want to outperform the competition, become 'employers of choice', and attract and retain the best and brightest, then a constructive, values-based culture must be fostered through planned and methodical change.

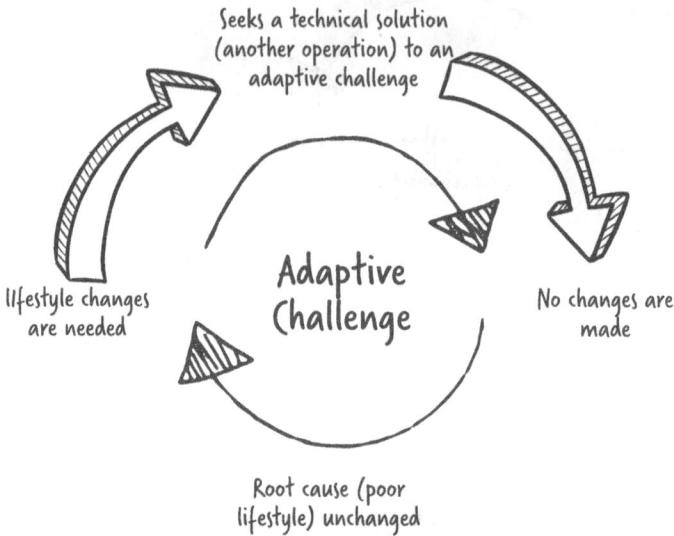

Figure 8: Problems arise when technical solutions are applied to adaptive challenges

Added to the toxic effects of passivity are the difficulties faced by managers when trying to solve tough challenges in today's world. Members of organisations, at all levels, often provide what has been called 'counterfeit leadership' (Williams, 2005), which is our topic for discussion in the next chapter.

Summary

We are stuck in the 'Age of Passivity', symbolised by people blaming others when things go wrong and not taking responsibility or being truly accountable.

In general, we rely too heavily on others to solve our problems, whether they are global issues like climate change, or those that confront us on a daily basis in organisations.

The 'Age of Passivity' means that because we rely on others for direction and solutions, we become passive, which means those in authority must provide even more direction and solve more of our problems for us.

Technical problems are relatively easy to fix because there are known (or knowable) solutions. Adaptive problems, on the other hand, require learning and a different approach that one person or entity can't fix alone.

CHAPTER 6

COUNTERFEIT LEADERSHIP

*There are some people who see a great deal and
some who see very little in the same things.*
—Thomas Henry Huxley

Technical versus Adaptive

The sad fact is that in organisations, valuable resources are squandered by managers and leaders who apply quick fixes (here's your pill) that don't work, or alternatively, misdiagnose the problem and so apply the wrong fix altogether. Dean Williams calls this 'counterfeit leadership' where the leader:

- Places an excessive emphasis on getting people to follow.
- Is pre-occupied with dominance as a control mechanism.
- Fails to fully engage the group and its many sub-groups.
- Is unwilling to look for solutions beyond their own comfort zone or the prevailing group paradigm.
- Believes they alone have the truth and know the way forward.

Managers and leaders don't necessarily do this on purpose or consciously, but one of the most common ways leaders provide counterfeit leadership is by applying a technical solution to an adaptive challenge. So, what's the difference?

A technical problem has a known solution that can be implemented with current know-how. It can be resolved through the application of authoritative expertise supported by the organisation's processes, policies and structures (Heifetz, et al., 2009). Adaptive challenges, on the other hand, can only be addressed through changes in people's priorities, values, beliefs, habits or loyalties. Progress lies beyond authoritative expertise to mobilise discovery and to shed old ways of looking at the problem.

Situation/Example	Counterfeit Leadership	Real Leadership
Dysfunctional behaviour exhibited by a senior member of the organisation	People ignore it, manage around it, or talk about it behind the person's back	Confront the behaviour directly with the person in a constructive and empathetic way
Underperforming business unit due to a culture of paternalism and nepotism	Merge the BU with another; provide technical training, re-structure the management team	Identify the root causal factors and address them; provide retraining; make hard calls about BU heads
Manager who gets short-term results but destroys value in the company and their people in the long-term	Reward the manager for delivering against company (six-monthly) short-term objectives	Provide coaching; performance management; remove if unable or unwilling to adapt and change
You attend meetings for your leadership team, where the tough issues are not discussed	You collude with the system by not raising these issues in the meetings	You raise issues in a constructive and assertive manner; ask the challenging questions
Your team or peers are not quite up to the job; not everyone is pulling their weight; people are afraid to try things in case they make a mistake	Jumping in and getting things done; not delegating appropriately; telling your team or peers what and how they should do things	Ensure people's motivation and capability meet the demands of the role through formal training, on-the-job upskilling, letting people experiment and learn more

Table 1: Counterfeit versus real leadership in organisations.

A real leader will:

- Get people to face reality as it relates to their condition, threats and opportunities.
- Mobilise the group to do adaptive work and adjust member values, habits, practices and priorities.
- Pursue the needed insight and wisdom to lead.
- Take responsibility for being the source of the movement.

Williams also summarises what real leadership is *not* about:

- Dominance or control.
- Putting a false set of tasks before people and getting them to follow.
- Getting one's own way and trying to get people to buy into something they are not ready to embrace, even if born of strong convictions and moral belief.
- Staying in your comfort zone and doggedly holding onto the world you know, even as the 'ship is sinking'.

Logical but Ineffective

While many leaders provide real leadership, many do not. I remember a time in my own life where I presided over a team that had very poor relationships with a support area. We needed them more than they needed us. Despite my efforts to resolve the problem, I failed. With hindsight and the passing of time, I can see that I contributed and perhaps even fed the problem. How? I took on the (traditional) management responsibility of doing 'the work' on behalf of the team. 'The work' was mostly logical. I had numerous conversations with the head of the support team, put processes and guidelines in place (an ineffective technical fix) and tried to build trust. All to no avail. What would have been a more constructive response? Think for a moment about what you would have done.

I should have created an environment where my own team and the support team were given responsibility to build relationships *themselves*, by creating more open and honest forums, as well as encouraging my team to take more positive action to demonstrate its commitment to making it work, ensuring that *all* the elephants (or what I like to call the 'undiscussibles') were on the table.

Summary

Treating adaptive challenges as if they were technical in nature is common, and leads to short-term fixes and long-term problems.

Technical challenges are those that are known or knowable.

Adaptive challenges require learning, and authority alone cannot solve them.

Counterfeit leadership describes the phenomenon of technical solutions being used to attempt to solve adaptive challenges. It looks like leadership is occurring, however, it isn't.

Real leadership is where the manager gets people to face the reality of their situation as well as mobilising people to do adaptive work.

When real leadership is effective, people take responsibility for being the source of the movement. Real leadership is not about exerting dominance or control, getting one's own way, getting people to buy in to something they are not ready to embrace, or staying in your comfort zone.

Sometimes because we are too personally invested in the challenge or situation, we may take action that doesn't allow for progress.

CHAPTER 7

THE DELUSION OF SOLUTIONS

The biggest mistake that leaders can make is to
give people false hope that melts like snow.
—Winston Churchill

False Promises, False Hope

In this chapter, rather than talk about counterfeit leadership broadly, I will focus primarily on the propensity of leaders to provide technical solutions to challenges that need an adaptive response (also counterfeit leadership). My thinking has been drawn from Williams, and the pioneering work of Heifetz, Grashow and Linsky.

Five Reasons Why Leaders Apply False Technical Solutions

Reason 1: The Seduction of Reward

The first reason for applying false (technical) solutions to adaptive challenges is that leaders who solve problems are rewarded by the organisation. After all, most managers and leaders have been previously successful by following this familiar pattern of solving problems quickly. In fact, many people in formal authoritative positions take great pride in labels like 'troubleshooter' or

'Mr Fixit'. Many have built their reputations on their ability to (apparently) solve problems over the long term.

Figure 9: The power of seduction can jeopardise doing the right thing

Those who provide effective solutions are rewarded through short and long term incentives, not to mention the ultimate honour of being called a leader. Whether we like to admit it, this seduction is like a 'banquet for the soul' and feeds our ego, sometimes to the point of being bloated. The risk is that we buy into the rhetoric around us so profoundly that we lose a level of self-awareness and connection with reality. I see evidence of this on a regular basis when providing feedback to leaders, based on the results of a development survey. For many, the gap between their self-perception and identity—and the way the world actually experiences them—can be like navigating a deep fissure in the dark.

My own team members (from the previous chapter) would praise, reward and reinforce my behaviour, often by saying what strong leadership I had displayed. This was, of course, very seductive. Who doesn't want to be called a leader? So I would repeat the types of behaviour that would let people off the hook by not having to confront the issues themselves.

Reason 2: Avoidance

The second reason leaders often apply false (technical) solutions to adaptive challenges is that it is much harder to confront the real, underlying issues than it is to apply a simplistic, known approach. It is much simpler to have a safe conversation about a superficial issue—one on which people collude and delude themselves into thinking is the real issue—than to confront the elephant in the room, team or organisation. When was the last time someone thanked you for pointing out a gap between their espoused values and those they actually demonstrate? It's not that likely.

Reason 3: Keeping the Temperature Tolerable

The third reason is that applying a technical solution keeps the temperature at lower levels, and people around them can stay in their comfort zones. The principles of adaptive leadership dictate that people and systems will act to maintain the status quo, and so will often avoid the real issue, conversation or decision that needs to be made. This is frankly how individuals, teams and whole organisations can stay 'stuck' by failing to address the real issues and challenges that reside within. It is, therefore, easier to avoid addressing the real problems that are affecting performance. People engage in very creative ways to avoid the prospect of change and the tension that comes with it. Leaders need to receive training on how to spot and then manage creative avoidance while, of course, not falling into the same trap by avoiding the work themselves.

Work avoidance strategies (adapted from Williams) include:

- *Blame, denial and shifting responsibility* (scapegoating) – examples include departments or divisions blaming the other one for delays.

- *Forming committees or working parties* – to analyse the problem ad nauseam, effectively delaying action. Alternatively, those in authority fail to divest any meaningful authority to the committee or working party, rendering it impotent (a favourite of governments where they are *seen* to be doing something) or delegate it to an outside party who can't do anything about it.

- *Personal attack or 'assassination'* – discredit the person trying to bring about change, move them on, take away the resources they need to continue, or in the worst case, literally 'take them out' (metaphorically). This could mean sacking them under the guise of incompetence or, in politics, metaphorically *assassinating* the person because of the change or cause they represented. There are many strategies leaders can be taught to help prevent this.

- *Focusing on the easier parts of the problem* that don't cause discomfort or too much stress. An example would be where a new technology solution is applied to lift customer service levels, while the real issue of poor quality management remains unaddressed.

- *Changing the scope of the project* or work to fit the current expertise or skill – projects or teams can retrofit the scope or breadth or work to fit with their current levels of comfort or mindset.

Reason 4: Managing Our Own Discomfort

The fourth reason we apply technical solutions to adaptive challenges is that our own discomfort level is kept within tolerable levels. I haven't met many people who enjoy 'confronting' reality, speaking the truth at great personal risk to themselves, or drawing attention to issues that are extremely sensitive – issues that people talk about at the water cooler but dare not mention in public. They require the creation of high levels of psychological safety if they are to be drawn out effectively.

Reason 5: Dancing on the Edge of Our Authority

The fifth and final reason why we apply false (technical) solutions to adaptive challenges is that, in order to lead adaptively, we actually have to dance on the edge of our authority.

The people who hired you or asked you to work on the project have certain expectations which define the boundaries of your formal and informal authority. Organisations reward people for staying right in the middle of their 'circle of authority'. It is only when we start to push those boundaries, challenge in areas where it is not necessarily welcomed, that we begin to truly lead adaptively. You won't be rewarded for pushing the boundaries or expanding your informal and formal circles of authority, but this is exactly what is needed.

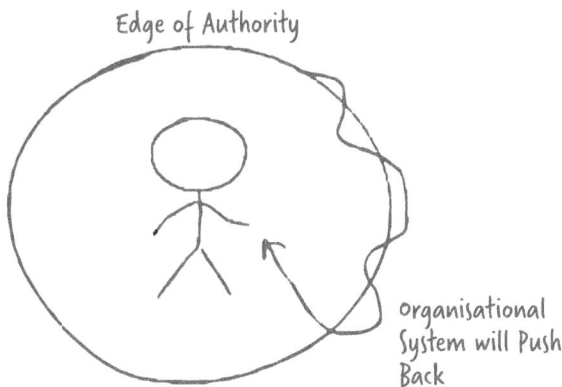

Figure 10: 'To lead is to live dangerously.' (Williams, 2005)

Real leadership requires courage, tenacity and a clear sense of oneself and what needs to change. While there are many languages and cultures with an interpretation for the actual word 'leadership', I have a favourite: the Indo-European root of the word leadership is *leith*, which means to go forth, to cross a threshold, or to die (Gerzon, 2003).

Figure 11: Root word for 'Leadership' demonstrates the risk

When going into battle, the solider carrying the flag at the front of the battalion was called the leader and he often was killed first, thereby warning the rest of the troops. I'm not suggesting we die on the sword for the cause. This isn't a very smart way to operate because then we're not around to continue the fight. What I am suggesting is that we need to let go of some of our fears. Once we overcome or work through the fear of stepping into the unknown, we are at the very heart and essence of leadership.

This takes courage, perseverance and resilience. It also means we sometimes need to act in ways that are counter to what our colleagues, and those more senior to us, expect. It may be that in order to move the system forward and demonstrate real leadership, we actually need to to meet the expectations of those around us at a rate they can tolerate. This is not how we are traditionally educated and trained to act in organisational life; however, it is exactly what may be needed.

Summary

Managers provide false technical solutions for five main reasons:

- Seduction or reward.
- Avoidance.
- To keep the temperature tolerable.
- To manage their own discomfort.
- Failing to dance on the edge of their authority.

To lead is to live dangerously. To make real change, we must learn to take calculated risks and be courageous.

We may need to incrementally fail to meet the expectations of stakeholders in order to make progress on important challenges.

PART 3:

A LEADERSHIP DECLARATION – OUR VISION FOR THE FUTURE

CHAPTER 8

A LEADERSHIP DECLARATION –
OUR VISION FOR THE FUTURE

Success is not final, failure is not fatal: it is the
courage to continue that counts.
—Winston Churchill

A Leadership Declaration

My Leadership Declaration aims to clearly state the case for leadership and its importance to all of us at this time. My declaration is as follows:

> Leadership is a shared relationship, where people are positively influenced to mobilise themselves around their toughest challenges, in service of a mutual purpose consistent with their fundamental values.

Why the World Needs Leaders Like You

Corporate Failure

We continue to witness corporate disasters attributed to a failure of leadership. An example is the Volkswagen emissions scandal that violated clean air rules in the US. The carmaker insisted that management was not aware of any cheating software, known as a defeat device, being used until shortly before the disclosure of the deception. It was later proven that management did have knowledge about the software (Boston & Wilkes, 2016).

In another example reported by *Fortune* magazine, Deutsche Bank was fined $2.5 billion in 2015 for rigging the worldwide market for short-term lending (and for obstructing the investigation into it by US and European regulators), and was fined €725 million for rigging Euribor, another interest rate benchmark, two years earlier (Smith, 2016).

And there was Wells Fargo, where, beginning in 2011, employees created about 1.5 million accounts and another half a million credit card accounts for the bank's existing customers resulting in charging customers fees for accounts they didn't know they had. There are literally hundreds of examples of failed and unethical leadership (McGrath, 2016).

Perhaps not surprisingly, trust in institutions is low while our expectations of leaders have stayed the same, if not increased. For example, Richard Edelman, in his annual measure of trust (the Edelman Trust Barometer) reported that in 2016 a deeply disturbing trend arose. He reported that a yawning trust gap is emerging between elite and mass populations. The global survey asks respondents how much they trust the four institutions of government, business, nongovernmental organisations and media to do what is right. The survey shows that trust is rising in the elite or 'informed public' group – those with at least a college education, who are very engaged in media, and have an income in the top 25 per cent. However, in the 'mass population' (85 per cent of the sample), trust levels have barely budged since the Great Recession (Edelman, 2009).

Unprecedented Global Disruption

Much has been written about the pace of change and its unrelenting nature. However, this comment doesn't necessarily pick up what is truly happening, and the potential impact on nations or the organisations that drive them.

Disruptive Forces

According to the 2015 report *No Ordinary Disruption*, the authors from the global consulting firm McKinsey assert that the world economy's operating system is being rewritten (Dobbs, et al., 2015). They assessed that during the Industrial Revolution, in the late 18th and early 19th centuries, one new force changed everything (industrialisation itself). Today, our world is undergoing an even more dramatic transition due to the confluence of four fundamental disruptive forces—the rise of emerging markets, the accelerating impact of technology on the natural forces of market competition, an aging world population, and accelerating flows of trade, capital, people, and data.

According to the authors, any one of these disruptive forces would rank among the greatest changes the global economy has ever seen. Compared with the Industrial Revolution, the authors estimate that this change is happening ten times faster and at 300 times the scale, or roughly 3,000 times the impact.

'Much as waves can amplify one another, these trends are gaining strength, magnitude, and influence as they interact with, coincide with, and feed upon one another.' (Dobbs, et al., 2015). Together, these four fundamental disruptive trends are producing monumental change.

Climate Change

Leadership in climate change, one of the world's most pressing adaptive challenges, remains patchy. Despite the 21st session of the

Conference of Parties (known as COP21) to the United Nations Framework Convention on Climate Change (UNFCCC) reaching a landmark agreement in December 2015, only real leadership being demonstrated by nations around the world will ensure a positive impact is felt in the future (Center For Climate Change Energy Solutions, 2015).

Prosperity

Similarly, according to the *World Bank's Poverty and Shared Prosperity Report 2016*, in 2013, the year of the latest comprehensive data on global poverty, 767 million people were estimated to have been living below the international poverty line of US$1.90 per person per day (World Bank, 2016). Almost 11 people in every 100 in the world, or 10.7 per cent of the global population were poor by this standard, about 1.7 percentage points down from the global poverty headcount ratio in 2012.

Despite decades of substantial progress in boosting prosperity and reducing poverty, the world continues to suffer from substantial inequalities. For example, the poorest children are four times less likely than the richest children to be enrolled in primary education across developing countries. Among the estimated 780 million illiterate adults worldwide, nearly two-thirds are women. Poor people face higher risks of malnutrition and death in childhood, and lower odds of receiving key health care interventions (World Bank, 2016).

The global issues we face will require unprecedented leadership and unprecedented levels of co-operation, concurrently, to mobilise communities and organisations.

A New Paradigm for the Future

To make progress on our most significant issues we need a new paradigm—one that inspires us to:

- Act constructively in a values-driven way.
- Empower each other to take responsibility and accountability at all levels of the organisation.
- Shift our focus from problem-centric to solution-centric (positive change).
- Make progress on the toughest issues and challenges.
- Create an environment of breakthrough performance, and high levels of commitment and learning.
- Liberate ourselves from old ways of thinking about how to manage and lead people.
- Develop systems intelligence.

As the industrial age wanes, new possibilities emerge to create a different paradigm of leadership. I propose a new paradigm that draws from many sources and builds on them in an integrative way. However, one doesn't change a paradigm by writing a book. The mechanistic, industrial paradigm has been in existence since the latter part of the 18th century and continues to shape society and modern organisations. It is a long, slow journey, yet incredibly worthwhile.

This is not a paradigm I claim to be inventing, but rather a paradigm that is emerging slowly after almost a 100-year stalemate. The essence of what I am proposing, however, has driven and continues to drive me and my colleagues to do this type of work. We are striving to create organisations that are more humanistic, where behaviour is values-driven and where each individual's potential and contribution can be optimised in service of the organisational mission which, in turn, should make a positive contribution to the world. We are interested in developing leaders from many different industries, fields and walks of life.

I should point out that I am not trying to provide the definitive answer on what leadership is and is not—people have been trying to do that for over 100 years. The words of Margaret Thatcher resonate when she said, 'To me, consensus seems to be the process of abandoning all beliefs, principles, values and policies. So it is something in which no one believes and to which no one objects (Margaret Thatcher Foundation, 1981).

My intention is to build a case for a new way of leading that incorporates a number of principles and leading schools of thought. Having begun my leadership declaration with a call for leaders to stand up and make a difference in the context of global challenges, the focus will now be firmly grounded in the organisational context, starting broadly and then becoming more focused on tangible and practical steps to lead more effectively or develop leaders to ensure the best chance of success. I am optimistic that you will apply many of the ideas in this book to your own organisation, as well other aspects of your life, whether it be as a parent, junior sports coach, or community leader. During the exploration, there will be opportunities to reflect and contextualise the discussion for your own situation.

Leadership and The Three Pillars of Performance

It would be remiss of me to discuss leadership development without putting it in a broader context. One of the models I have adapted to guide clients is a relatively simple one from Michael Beer (Beer, 2009).

Organisations that are able to deliver sustained performance have developed the three pillars of:

- Performance alignment.
- Psychological alignment.
- Capacity for learning and change.

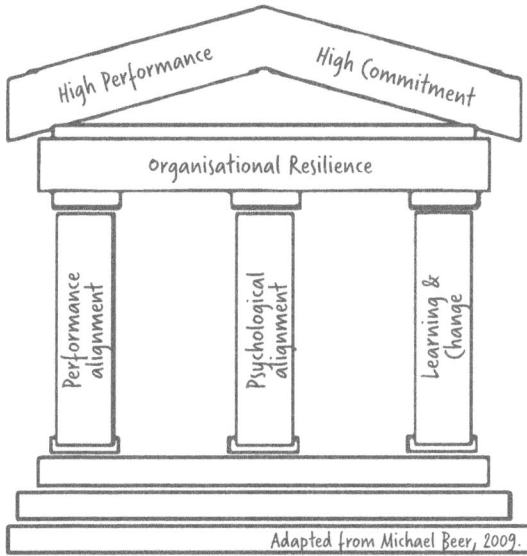

Figure 12: Three pillars of performance

Performance alignment occurs when the total organisational system, including systems, structures, people and culture, fits performance goals and strategy. *Psychological alignment* is the emotional attachment people have at all levels—particularly key business unit leaders—to the purpose, mission and values of the organisation *(I just love working here,* is heard a lot).

If the organisation is to sustain both performance and psychological alignment, it must also have the capacity for learning and change (Beer, 2009).

The three pillars provide organisational resilience to rapid change and uncertainty. Those organisations strong in all three, markedly increase their chances of sustaining high performance and high commitment—sometimes over decades. Southwest Airlines is cited as a company that has achieved this over a period of four decades. While competitors were able to copy some aspects of the three pillars, they were never able to achieve psychological alignment or the capacity to learn and change.

In terms of the capacity for learning and change, 'The only enduring source of competitive advantage is an organisation's relative ability to learn faster than its competition', wrote former head of planning at Shell (de Geus, 1988). For de Geus, learning was 'the process whereby an organisation evolved to remain in harmony with a changing environment', and was key to success. We are facing unprecedented change and learning challenges that require agility and a new kind of systems awareness and adaptability.

In terms of psychological alignment, relationships and teamwork become central drivers of behaviour, with people sacrificing their immediate self-interest for the demanding goals required of high performance. In effect, organisations seeking psychological alignment consciously develop a 'psychological contract': a high investment, high return exchange between the firm and its employees.

Leading 'With', Not Leading 'Over'

The discussion about relationships and teams being central drivers for high performance organisations flows nicely into the idea that leadership is about 'leading with' rather than 'leading over'. This has been explored previously by people such as Burns and Rost (Burns, 1978, Hollander, 1978 and Rost, 1993).

Drawing on Rost as a building block, leadership is viewed *not* as something that is done to others, but rather as a relationship *with* others. Of course, the word follower becomes a problem if we dispense with the traditional notion of leader/follower. While Rost settled on calling followers 'collaborators', I will simply refer to them collectively as 'team'. While perhaps not precise in terms of what a team really is, I find it less clumsy than other terms.

Rost's definition of leadership then becomes an influence relationship among leaders and team members who intend real changes that reflect their mutual purposes. This definition of leadership includes four essential elements:

1. The leader-team relationship is based on influence and is multidirectional. It is non-coercive because the relationship would turn into an authority, power, or dictatorial relationship if coercive behaviours were used to gain compliance.

2. Leaders and team members are the people in this relationship. If leadership is what the relationship is, then team members *and* formal leaders are all 'doing leadership'. All leadership relationships need not look (or be) the same.

3. Leaders and team members intend real changes. The word 'intend' means the changes the leaders and team promote are purposeful, that the changes didn't happen by chance or accident. Change should be substantive, significant or transforming.

4. The leader and team members' intended changes reflect their mutual purposes. The changes must not only reflect what the leaders want, but also what team members want.

Rost's definition clearly distinguishes leadership from management, not only because of the people who are possible leaders (thus, managers are not automatically leaders and non-managers can be leaders), but in the three other essential elements required for leadership: influence, intended real change, and mutual purposes. None of those three elements are essential to management.

Management	Leadership
Authority relationship	Influence relationship
Done by managers and subordinates	Done by leaders and team members
Involves coordinating people and resources to produce and sell goods /services in an organisation	Involves leaders and team members intending real changes in an organisation
Coordinated activities reflect the organisation's purpose	Reflects mutual purposes
Requires a position/role from which to operate	Anyone can lead from anywhere in the organisation
Constrains people based on how it has traditionally been done	Mobilises people to find new and better ways to do things

Table 2: Contrast *between* management and leadership

The intention here is not to denigrate management but to distinguish it from leadership. Management plays a vital function in all organisations and societies. We need both management and leadership in organisations and societies to survive and prosper.

Adaptive Leadership

Adaptive leadership, pioneered by Ron Heifetz and Marty Linsky over a period of 30 years at Harvard University's John F. Kennedy School of Government, characterises leadership as something that is 'exercised' (Linksy & Heifetz, 2002) and complements the principles outlined by Rost. It is, therefore, much easier to discuss leadership as an action, and not a position. Those who lead in this sense don't need to rely on the constraints of formal authority or positional power.

Heifetz believes that we have confused authority with leadership for too long. It's actually a contradiction in terms to say, 'the leadership isn't exercising any leadership'. What we should say is, 'people in authority aren't exercising any leadership'. There are many people who are skilled at gaining formal and informal authority, but never lead. If leadership differs from the capacity to gain authority and, therefore, a 'following', what anchors us in leadership?

Leadership takes place in the context of problems and challenges; it becomes even more critical in the face of enduring challenges. The current ways of doing things become obsolete and, therefore, new and innovative ways must be discovered.

In their excellent book, *The Practice of Adaptive Leadership: Tools and Tactics for Changing Your Organisation and the World*, Heifetz, Grashow and Linsky define leadership in this way: "Adaptive leadership is the practice of mobilizing people to tackle tough challenges and thrive."

The elements that particularly resonate are:

- Practice – as discussed, leadership is not a role or position, it is an action. The word practice indicates an ongoing activity.

- Mobilising – this is at the heart of adaptive leadership. Mobilising people to take responsibility and action locally. It speaks to many of the problems discussed with the industrial paradigm of leadership.

- People – people are the only ones who can innovate to help the organisation become more productive and achieve its strategy.

- Tough challenges – there are many problems and challenges in organisations, many of which can be solved through the application of normal management practices and systems. Tough challenges indicate those that require a different approach, and will promote breakthrough performance.

- Thrive – just as with biological systems, organisational systems and human systems need to adapt and become stronger to meet future challenges. This is more than just survival.

Adaptive leadership demands learning, where values, beliefs and priorities need to change in order to make progress. It is where the application of technical solutions will not fix the problem and requires a response outside the current repertoire. With adaptive challenges, the people with the problem are the problem *and* the solution. Adaptive work often requires more of an experimental approach, so the timeframes are often longer.

In our earlier example with the doctor, if he or she was to show adaptive or real leadership, what might they do? Imagine a cardiac surgeon, for example, telling patients that they will refuse to do the operation unless patients do their part of the work – quit smoking, exercise, adopt a healthy diet. Also, to ensure compliance, the surgeon insists the patient place 50 per cent of their assets into a holding account for six months pending their successful change. It is likely most will find another surgeon who will do the operation and let them off the hook (Heifetz, et al., 2009). We let people off the hook in organisations constantly.

Our surgeon was demonstrating adaptive leadership by getting the patient to take responsibility for making healthy lifestyle changes rather than simply expecting the operation would fix all their woes. Without the deeper-level change, the patient will be back for another operation in the future, or worse. Could your organisation benefit from people taking full responsibility and accountability for their own problems rather than deferring upwards? I haven't found an organisation yet where this aspect doesn't need work. We're often so used to dealing with each other in ways that are less than 100 per cent accountable, that we sometimes forget what it actually feels like when people are 100 per cent accountable. It's refreshing and it greases the wheels of business like almost nothing else.

Leaders who get the most attention in the media are those who act like leadership is all about them. 'You'd think that the sheep were only there for the benefit of the shepherd.' (Heifetz, 1999).

It's useful to point out that traditional roles and functions are not lost in this way of operating. In fact, Burns argues that it enhances leadership because, '... leadership electrifies the system as followers become leaders and vice versa' (Burns, 1978).

The best form of leadership, therefore, generates other leaders, not followers (Beer, 2009). And so one of the most important functions of leadership is to create an environment of high psychological safety.

Google, for example, in its quest to build the perfect team, studied 180 teams (called Project Aristotle) from all over the company to determine what the key success factors might be (Duhigg, 2016). After looking at all of the teams for more than a year, researchers concluded that understanding and influencing group norms were the keys to improving Google's teams. But the researchers needed to figure out which norms mattered most. Within psychology, researchers sometimes colloquially refer to traits like 'conversational turn-taking' and 'average social sensitivity' as aspects of what's known as psychological safety. When the researchers from Google came across the term, it all made sense.

To feel 'psychologically safe' we must know that we can be free enough, sometimes, to share the things that scare us without fear of recrimination. We must be able to talk about what is messy or sad, to have hard conversations with colleagues who are driving us crazy. We can't be focused just on efficiency. This should be the goal of anyone responsible for people.

A New Leadership Paradigm

If we integrate the thinking and principles of Rost (leadership is a relationship), Beer (Three Pillars of Performance), and Heifetz and Laurie (adaptive leadership), we can see a great deal of commonality and power. The essential elements of leadership then become:

1. Leadership is about the relationship.

2. Anyone can lead from anywhere in the organisation.

3. Leadership is about influencing and mobilising people.

The action of leadership involves real change to make progress on tough challenges to serve a mutual purpose.

Current Paradigm	New Paradigm
Leaders are smarter than everyone else	Everyone can contribute in a meaningful way
Leaders have the answers	The answer resides in the collective, not individuals
Leaders are active while followers are passive	All employees are engaged and contributing
Leaders need to motivate their charges	People are self-motivated if given the opportunity
Followers need to be given direction to be productive	Employees can be very productive if the right environment exists
Leadership can be elitist and special	Leadership is a relationship
Leadership is individualistic	Leadership is shared

Vertical leadership – top-down philosophy, where the leader is decisive, efficient, unemotional and in-control	Horizontal leadership – collaborative, power-sharing facilitation and empowerment
Objective, single, mechanical, hierarchical and controllable	The world is more subjective, complex, diverse, mutually shaping and spontaneously changing
Vertical communication reinforces command and control	Horizontal communication fosters the free flow of information and collaboration
Focus is on problems and deficits	Focus is on solutions and strengths

Table 3: Contrasting the current paradigm with a new paradigm of leadership

My definition of leadership is not meant to be a pithy one-liner, but rather a statement that captures the essence of what I think is important for the future of organisations and the planet. At an organisational level, there is little doubt that real leadership is the 'engine room' of performance. In the absence of systemic, results-focused leadership, breakthrough performance and high commitment will not be achieved.

Dee Hock perhaps sums up this definition when he says, 'The most abundant, least expensive, and most constantly abused resource in the world is human ingenuity. The source of that abuse is mechanistic, Industrial Age, dominator concepts of organisations and the management practices they spawn.(Hock, 1999).'

Everyone was born a leader until we were sent to school and taught to be managed, to manage and comply. You will remember my opening story where you were either the leader or the follower. It was unheard of to have two leaders. Today, far too often, we manage things and people in exactly the same way, the way we've done it since the 19th century. It's time for a new reality.

The new paradigm is about tapping into the potential we all have, including the desire to make a significant contribution. This call for a new paradigm is beyond surviving to something much grander. Covey describes it as 'tapping into the higher reaches of human genius and motivation' (Schein, 2006). It is the intersection of people's talents (your natural gifts and strengths), passion (those things that naturally energise, excite and inspire you), needs (including what your organisation or the world needs from you) and conscience (what you know to be the right thing to do).

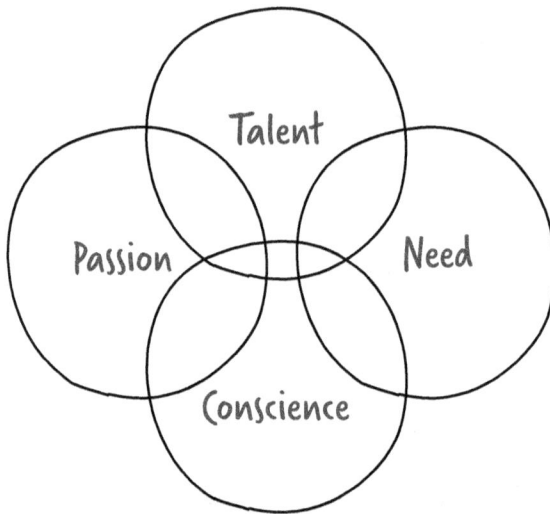

Figure 13: Tapping into the higher reaches of human genius and motivation (Covey, 2006)

A new paradigm must place more value and emphasis on leveraging strengths while managing our weaknesses. For example, positive psychology literature demonstrates there is very little evidence to support the value of aspiring to become a 'well-rounded' leader. No-one became extraordinary by trying to be good at everything. In organisations, and in the community generally, we must each play a role to help people tap into their dormant or under-utilised talents and strengths.

Leadership is when people communicate to others their worth and potential so clearly they will come to see it in themselves (Schein, 2006).

Despite a person's accomplishments, it seems that all of us have a little (or a lot) of the imposter syndrome (Clance & Imes, 1978)—a psychological phenomenon in which people are unable to internalise their accomplishments. I often mention this in programs, and without exception, at least half the room will nod in agreement, laugh nervously or give me a meek smile. I mention imposter syndrome to groups because if leadership is truly about enabling others to succeed, don't they deserve a fair dose of belief from those they work with? If we don't feel a degree of competence and confidence in ourselves, it is less likely that we will affirm and grow others effectively. Instead, we will expend unnecessary time, energy and mental headspace proving to the world how accomplished we are.

Carol Dweck writes elegantly about fixed versus growth mindset (Dweck, 2006). People with fixed mindsets believe qualities like intelligence or talent are fixed traits, and so invest time and energy into confirming and proving their existence to the world and that talent alone equals success. However, people with a growth mindset believe that their most basic abilities can be developed through dedication and hard work, thereby creating a value for learning and growth.

I have been fortunate to have at least two work colleagues and friends in my life who have done exactly this – they demonstrated a growth mindset in themselves and in me. At different times, they both had a greater belief in my potential and capability than I had in myself. For example, one manager said, "Phil, I think you're cruising. You can be anything you want to be in this organisation, such is your potential." What do you think happened to my confidence and self-belief as a result? They changed the course of my career and life in a positive and inspiring way. What a simple, yet impactful leadership action. Has someone provided you with a similar gift? Or perhaps a more challenging question: have you provided such a gift?

What You Should Know About Leadership and Management Development

It is also true that both management and leadership development go hand-in-hand, thus there are often benefits in combining management and leadership development programs. After all, good leaders do not set aside their leadership skills when they focus on the managerial aspects of the enterprise, nor do good managers set aside their managerial skills when they focus on the leadership side of the enterprise. Since both can be extremely complex processes, it is often hard to say where one begins and the other one ends (Changing Minds, 2009).

Here, I would like to provide several recommendations and guidelines for those responsible for leadership development programs:

1. Ensure leadership development doesn't occur in a vacuum. Leadership and management development should align with (1) a values-based culture, which every organisation should be striving for, and (2) is fit-for-purpose, for example, builds capacity to execute the organisation's strategy. Leadership development needs to be framed and grounded in terms of the leader's biggest challenges, not an ephemeral burst of euphoria from short, superficial interventions. This represents an 'outside-in' approach where the organisation's context (including market, community, etc.) is considered and well understood, so the organisational strategy can be formulated based on the organisation's vision and mission, in order to formulate the type of leadership needed.

2. Always build organisational capacity around the Three Pillars of Performance. Development programs need to be firmly grounded within (1) Capacity for Learning and Change, (2) Performance Alignment, and (3) Psychological Alignment. If your development programs aren't grounded in the three pillars (or closely-aligned principles), the return-on-investment you deserve probably won't be realised.

3. Ensure programs are well balanced with a healthy bias towards self-management. The most effective programs teach participants as much about themselves as gaining valuable practical skills, including building trust, leading high performance teams, and strengthening emotional intelligence (see the Seven Spheres of Leadership Mastery model in Part 4).

4. Involve key stakeholders in design, including executive members, managers of participants (those who will be attending the program) and some of the participants themselves, to raise awareness, excitement and engagement. Depending on your organisation and situation, you may even consider obtaining customer input.

5. Stop focusing on the leader. Leadership programs that only attempt to produce leader qualities among participants are less useful. Programs must reach well beyond emphasising leader traits, behaviours, and personal characteristics (Rost, 1993).

6. Prepare participants to use influence within non-coercive relationships. Program activities should train participants to use persuasive and rational strategies of influence (Rost, 1993).

7. Help participants understand the nature of transformational change. Leadership development programs should illustrate the key role organisational change plays in the post-industrial view of leadership. As change agents, participants should learn to challenge the status quo, create new visions, and sustain the movement (Rost, 1993).

8. Reconstruct participants' basic view toward a collaboration orientation. Encourage participants to challenge the basic assumptions about life that are based on self-interest and competition. Leadership in the new millennium is much more collaborative and, therefore, leadership programs should encourage consensus, cooperation, and collaboration rather than competition and unhelpful conflict (Rost, 1993).

9. Make development an everyday activity. Much has been written about the best way to develop managers and leaders. There is also growing discontent that many of the current development practices simply don't work, despite the leadership development industry being a multi-billion dollar industry. Many organisations are working to 'crack the code'. I believe that 'Learning & Development 2.0' will focus on connecting formal and informal learning through leader-led conversations. The work we do increasingly with organisations is training managers to have leader-led, focused conversations that have a business or team issue at their core, while developing people at the same time. We use an online Accountability Engine that helps drive and support the right behaviours.

Our Driving Goal

If it is our goal to prepare those who work in our organisations, governments and communities to lead effectively in the 21st century, then we must embrace this new paradigm in order to be successful in a world where rapid and constant change is the new 'status quo'.

Our leadership programs should promote and foster learning, adaptability, openness, authenticity, and the skills required to live leadership as a relationship and shared journey. Anything less and we will be selling ourselves, our employees and society short.

Summary

The world needs leaders like you, now more than ever. There is much work to do in equality, prosperity, climate change and in organisations generally.

There are four key disruptive forces affecting the world today, any one of these disruptive forces would rank among the greatest changes the global economy has ever seen.

To make progress on our most significant issues, we need a new paradigm that inspires us to act differently.

My intention in writing this book is to build a case for a new way of leading that incorporates a number of principles and leading schools of thought.

The new paradigm is about tapping into the potential in all of us, including the desire to make a significant contribution.

Organisations that are able to deliver sustained performance have developed the three pillars: performance alignment, psychological alignment, and capacity for learning and change.

Leadership is a shared relationship, where people are positively influenced to mobilise themselves around their toughest challenges, in service of a mutual purpose consistent with fundamental values.

Leadership development is a thriving industry, yet the benefits of traditional methods are questionable. Organisations need and deserve a much more thoughtful way to develop today's leaders and our next generation of leaders.

PART 4:

THE SEVEN
SPHERES
OF LEADERSHIP
MASTERY

CHAPTER 9

THE SEVEN SPHERES OF LEADERSHIP MASTERY

If your actions inspire others to dream more, learn more,
do more and become more, you are a leader.
—John Quincy Adams

A Leadership Development Framework

The Seven Spheres of Leadership Mastery is a central model used in my consulting practice. It is based on research, leadership theories, models and experience in working with leaders. It provides a touchstone for leadership development and practice, rather than a definitive list of required qualities and attributes. The principles and depth that underpin each sphere have helped thousands of leaders and organisations be more successful. Based on each organisational context, strategy and challenge, programs are customised at individual, team and organisational levels. We have found that the seven spheres contribute powerfully to many of the ideas and themes outlined in this book, so when you read them they act as a summary, rather than an abundance of new information.

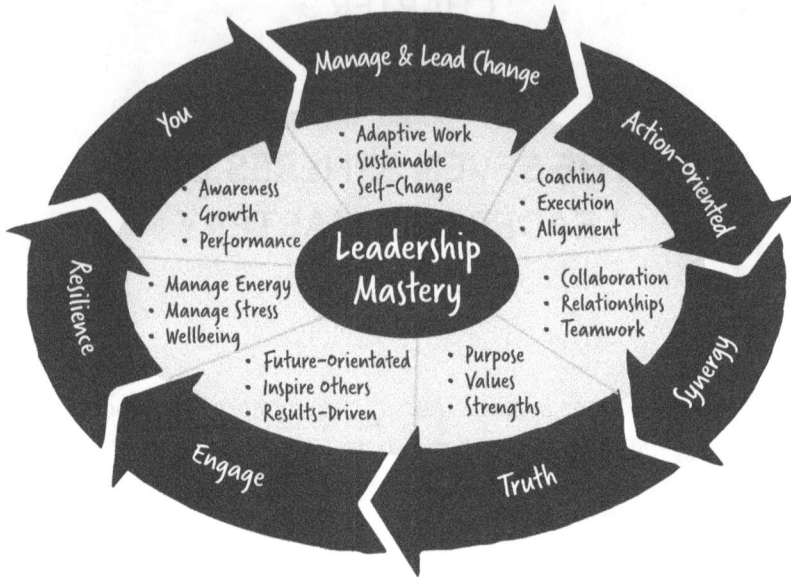

Figure 14: The seven spheres of leadership mastery

What follows is a short description of each sphere, when in Part 5, they are brought to life through a rolling case study.

Manage and Lead Change

Key words and phrases: agility, trusting self, manage and lead change, influencing, problem to an opportunity, learning, self-change, transition and systems intelligence.

The ability to manage and lead change is an ongoing demand on leaders. There is nothing truer than the statement *change is constant*. In fact, disequilibrium is the new normal. Research shows that the number one issue facing senior leaders is dealing with adaptive challenges and ambiguity. Adaptive challenges can be defined as those without a defined solution, that require fundamental changes in values and beliefs and where there are often legitimate yet competing perspectives emerging (Heifetz, et al., 2009).

Adaptive problems are often systemic problems with no ready answers, and therefore systems intelligence (the ability to see the system and patterns of interdependence) can be useful. To effectively lead change in this environment, leaders need a special set of skills and approaches. Skills include *getting on the balcony* (big picture perspective) and the ability to identify adaptive challenges (versus technical), regulating distress, maintaining disciplined attention, giving work back to where it belongs and protecting the voices of leadership below (Cashman, 2008).

Decisions about change are clustered into two archetypal theories and strategies for change, neither of which are sufficient on their own (Beer, 2009): *Theory E*, which focuses on creating economic value, while *Theory O* focuses on developing organisational capabilities and culture. Leaders are encouraged to embrace the paradox sometimes created by both archetypes, called the *third strategic choice*. This integrative strategy has the benefits of short-term financial performance as well as long-term benefits of sustained change in all three pillars of performance.

I am constantly surprised, when working with organisations, at how many senior people fail to consider both E and O strategies concurrently. I once worked with a professional services firm (primarily on culture change). The HR Director insisted on telling me that the organisation needed to get a major systems implementation finalised before they could re-commence culture change efforts. What he failed to realise was that everything that happens in organisations – including behaviours, tolerated or not tolerated, system design, or policy and process improvement – is a culture change opportunity. They are implicitly interdependent – full stop!

Positive change requires letting go of old patterns and taking a fresh perspective. It includes a focus on opportunities rather than problems, long-term versus short-term. and adaptability versus control. It also invites us to move away from a problem-centric focus (that we love so much in organisations) to a solution-centric focus. Do you spend your energy and attention on what's not working, rather than on what you want to create in the future?

Action-Oriented

> Key words and phrases: coaching (self and others), potential, influencing, alignment, awareness, acceptance, commitment, action.

The sound execution of strategy, combined with effective change management, is essential for success. While many leaders and teams develop sound plans and strategies, few actually execute them effectively. The notion of entropy (a loss or leakage of energy in a system) is of particular concern. This is where teams work on the wrong things, or on the right things, but ineffectively.

I worked with a team that became very excited by the Critical Success Factors (CSFs) that had been formulated at their team off-site. Despite my recommendations to establish support mechanisms (that is, a managed project plan) to ensure they were properly implemented, the CEO failed to see the need. Twelve months later, the team had barely moved on with what they said a year earlier was critical to their success, and the business was languishing.

While entropy can be minimised through alignment, too much alignment can actually be counter-productive. Alignment shouldn't equal frozen. In executing strategy or daily operations, there needs to be adaptability and flexibility built into the system, including a cultural norm that gives people permission at all levels to challenge and question the status quo. Within this context, formal leaders need to create an environment where others can successfully align behaviours, symbols and systems to help ensure that valuable resources are used effectively and efficiently. Aligning people, processes and systems behind the vision also ensures sustainable and meaningful change in the service of business goals – the holy grail of organisational success.

At the individual level, leadership is about creating a safe environment to enable others to fulfil their potential – in effect, be their best. It's about coaching others, rather than trying to control them, drawing out talents and strengths in the service of the team and organisational objectives. The Action-Oriented Sphere is also about self-coaching, where we take responsibility for enhancing our own self-awareness, accepting new information, committing to change where appropriate, and then taking definitive and stepwise action towards the goal.

Synergy

> Key words and phrases: relationships, collaboration, constructive conflict, managing teams, service, power, presence, emotional intelligence.

Leaders create synergy by building meaningful relationships and high levels of trust. Importantly, research demonstrates that the most effective leaders have competencies in both interpersonal skills as well as a focus on results (Beer, 2009). We also know that sometimes leaders must give up some of their *relational equity* in the service of something bigger. Leaders need to be able to bring critical issues to the surface and deal with conflict constructively. Apart from courage, this requires leaders to be emotionally intelligent, highly self-aware and tuned in to those around them.

Formal leaders also need to be able to make the shift from producing results to enabling and empowering others to produce the results. This is often a difficult transition for leaders to make, because they need to let go of what made them successful in the past—technical competence. Once leaders begin to make this transition, they also begin to realise that the key role of leadership is to serve the needs of others' success, not the opposite. The shepherd exists for the sheep, not the other way around.

Navigating the 'leadership transition' is one of the most common areas in which I am requested to engage. Whether it be partners in law and accounting firms, investment bankers or more generalist roles, making the transition from technician to leader is difficult. I have found that a lot of the success we enjoy in supporting people to make this transition is to re-frame leadership around key business challenges. In other words, leadership development occurs in the context of their (work) reality, not in a vacuum. New leaders and high potentials begin to clearly see how they can lead effectively and leverage their technical skills, concurrently. Leadership, however, becomes their new benchmark of success.

Underpinning the Synergy Sphere is the power of presence, the quality of absolute attention and listening. Presence can inspire and energise others and help them realise their potential.

Truth

> Key words and phrases: purpose, values, legacy, talents, strengths, making a difference, authenticity.

Truth is about connecting with our purpose, values and core strengths in areas that make a difference. Purpose is not a goal or the latest fad; it's something leaders need to discover, and is beyond our job or even career. It includes a reason for being that drives action beyond oneself. It is only with this clarity that extraordinary performance can occur, in both business and personal arenas. Values, on the other hand, are the standards and guiding principles that govern our lives.

In my experience, values are often talked about in organisations, particularly when everything is going well. But when there are real business challenges to confront, values are considered last. An exception was a Managing Director in the Asia Pacific region. She would regularly talk about the organisational values and use them as a reference in making tough decisions. Sometimes the values clashed directly with each other (for example, customer and shareholder), but it was the robust conversations surrounding the values that made the team's decision-making processes so effective.

Strengths enable us to be our best by leveraging what we're good at and extinguishing our weaknesses. Truth means being congruent and authentic in service of what we believe in as leaders. These three domains form a powerful coalition (Schein, 2006).

Inspiring leaders openly communicate their principles and what they stand for, despite their popularity. Most importantly, they model the behaviours required to move towards a high-performance culture. They truly 'walk the talk' in everything they do. If you influence the lives of those around you, you are engaging in the act of leadership. Each of us is creating a legacy as we live our lives. Our leadership legacy is the sum total of the difference we make in people's lives. Many leaders fail to consciously craft their legacy, instead, leaving it to chance.

Engage

Key words and phrases: vision, future orientation, goals, influencing, inspire, storytelling.

Leaders need to be able to create a compelling vision, or picture of the future, that creates a highly focused, results-driven culture. An organisation's vision must be a picture that energises people rather than just a 'let's-go-through-the-motions' type statement. Telling the story about a compelling mission, vision and values can energise entire organisations, when done well. While most leaders love to make strategy, it is a well-crafted vision and supporting values that spawn strategic action. The absence of a vision will doom any strategy—especially a strategy for change.

Do you want to encourage extraordinary performance? Do you want people to do great things? If the answer is yes, then create a culture that inspires, empowers and energises people. People will only do what they have to do for a manager who does not display leadership, but they will always give their best for a manager who is a real leader. To inspire, you must both create resonance and move people with a compelling vision. You must embody what you ask of others, and be able to articulate a shared vision in a way that inspires others to act. You must offer a sense of common purpose beyond the day-to-day tasks, making work exciting and fun.

While being an inspiring leader is insufficient on its own, those who are able to connect powerfully with people are at a distinct advantage. Often, people can feel inspired in unexpected or counter-intuitive ways. It is not the heroic leader who usually inspires others, but rather the simple human actions such as authenticity, empathy, or a powerful personal story. These qualities can be used to mobilise people, connect with others, and build quality relationships.

Resilience

> Key words and phrases: energy management, wellbeing, optimiom, stress management, exercise.

Sound energy management practices help people to achieve sustained performance, energy and enjoyment. Traditional views have addressed only parts of the energy management equation. Sound energy management means addressing all four domains effectively—physical, emotional, mental and spiritual (head, heart, body, meaning). A very simple personal story will help illustrate the power of tapping into these energy sources for ourselves and others.

When my son Thomas was about nine years old, each school morning we had to go through a protracted and frustrating ritual of waking him up from a sleep deeper than *Sleeping Beauty*. On Saturday nights, however, he would sleep dressed in his football gear (except boots) to 'save time' on Sunday mornings, so he wouldn't be late for football. Thomas would get up at around 5 am (strangely, unassisted) on Sundays and would wake me at 6 am (for football at 9 am). This is the power of the fourth energy source—spiritual (purpose and meaning). Can you imagine the power of tapping into this energy source for yourself, and those in your organisation?

Energy management is not limited to oneself. Effective leaders also know how to unlock energy and potential in others through an empowering, strengths-based approach. The field of positive psychology holds significant promise for how we manage and lead in organisations. The Values-In-Action (VIA) survey is a great starting point to think about your own strengths and how to leverage them.

While 'life balance' remains distinctly individual, having the requisite skills to manage all four domains is fundamental to sustained, high performance. In today's fast-paced world, where it feels like we're being pulled in many different directions, energy management and building resourcefulness are critical.

You

> Key words and phrases: character, authenticity, self-change, beliefs, self-awareness.

Many people tend to split the act of leadership from the person, whereas the two are inseparable. We also tend to see leadership as an external event; something we do. Leadership, however, comes from a deeper reality; it comes from our values, principles, life experiences and essence. It is a whole-of-person action. We lead by virtue of who we are—this is real leadership (or leadership from the inside out). Fundamental to the most effective, results-producing leaders are authenticity, influence and value creation (Cashman, 2008), (Schein, 2006).

My definition of leadership is that it is a shared relationship where people are positively influenced to mobilise themselves around their toughest challenges, in the service of a mutual purpose consistent with fundamental values. Leadership can come from our character, the essence of who we are; or it can come from a pattern of coping, where we tend to react to circumstances to elicit an immediate result.

Character is the essence of a leader and works to transform and open up possibilities and potential, while coping protects us and helps us get through challenging circumstances. If used sparingly, it has value. The coping leader may get results, but also exhibit defensiveness, fear, withdrawal, or a desire to win at all costs – all things that *diminish* performance (Schein, 2006).

Like most people who have worked in organisations for a period of time, I have experienced both 'character and coping-based' leaders. Those who lead through character are generally those who also manage 'task' and 'relationship' most effectively.

I coached a CEO from a not-for-profit organisation who was the epitome of a character-based leader. He consciously focused on living in accord with his principles and values. He had a deep sense of purpose and legacy, and he cared about the community and the role of his organisation within it. He was not threatened by his executive team or those who demonstrated superior knowledge, skills or experience. His belief in people and his role in developing them is captured in a quote from Wilma Rudolph, the first female American runner to win three gold medals at a single Olympics:

> 'Never underestimate the power of dreams and the influence of the human spirit. We are all the same in this notion: The potential for greatness lives within each of us'.

Summary

The Seven Spheres of Leadership Mastery is a central model to help understand best practice leadership development and the practice of leadership.

The seven evidenced-based areas include: Manage and Lead Change, Action-Oriented, Synergy, Truth, Engage, Resilience and You.

The Seven Spheres of Leadership Mastery provide a useful summary for many of the ideas and themes in this book and can be used as a touchstone to think about your own leadership.

CHAPTER 10

LEADERSHIP IN PRACTICE

Leadership and learning are indispensable to each other.
—John Fitzgerald Kennedy

Maintain and Develop Systems Intelligence

We have discussed a number of trends and themes surrounding the current industrial age leadership paradigm. I have called for a shift from the current paradigm to a new paradigm based on relationships, empowerment, autonomy, adaptability and action. Now it is time to outline what we can do, in a practical sense, to bring this new paradigm to life.

'Systems intelligence is the ability to see the systems and patterns of interdependence within organisations and beyond' (Schein, 2006). Once people start to see the systemic patterns, early action can be taken. Edgar Shein believes human systems are essentially role networks, and one must learn to influence roles more than people. In the work we do with leaders, either in a one-on-one coaching capacity, leadership or team development, we use systems maps and role analysis extensively. Focusing on your role, and the role an individual is playing, can be extraordinarily powerful.

For example, once when working with an executive team, one member drew his systems map using the metaphor of a car, *with him as the brake.* This created a rich discussion about the role that person felt they needed to play to protect the organisation from undue risk. It created a major breakthrough in the team as they were able to have a deep discussion about the issue and move to a whole new plane of performance.

Give the Work Back to the People Who Have the Problem

I remember coaching the newly-appointed Chairman of a large Australian-based organisation. During a discussion he outlined how he had scheduled a 'meet and greet' tour of all their offices around the country. During the tour, he intended to talk to as many staff as possible to get their views on what was happening in the firm – both good and bad. Good so far, right? When I asked him the purpose of doing that, he said that this would enable him to work out all the things he needed to do to fix the organisation (along with the CEO and her team).

The Chairman was about to fall into the common trap of shouldering the burden of all the ills of the organisation. While he certainly has a responsibility and, along with the CEO, is ultimately accountable, this doesn't mean he had to take on the responsibility of fixing it single-handedly—an impossible task. Consider 'who has the monkey on their back?' The monkey is analogous to thinking about who either (1) retains the problem, challenge or issue, or (2) effectively hands it to someone else. People are very good at handing the monkey to those in authority.

We discussed some simple alternate strategies such as:

1. When asking people what's not working, ask them what they have tried in the past to make progress on the problem.

2. Ask them what support they need from you to make this happen.

3. Ask them what type of organisation they would like to help create.

Listen to Those Who Don't Sing from the Same Page

'Organisations are coercive systems.' (Schein, 2006). They tend to reinforce a party line, so listening to the periphery, those who do not share the views of the mainstream, is a skill leaders will need more and more as there will be limited understanding, at best, of the forces shaping culture. Heifetz and Laurie also talk about 'protecting the leadership voices from below' (Heifetz & Laurie, 2001).

Whistle-blowers, creative deviants and those who call attention to things people would rather ignore, *are routinely smashed and silenced in organisations*. They generate disequilibrium, and the best way for companies to silence them is to neutralise them, often in the name of 'alignment' or teamwork. I have regularly heard CEOs and other senior members *deride* certain vocal members in their businesses. These vocal individuals may well be speaking directly to systemic issues that need to be addressed.

Create Psychological Safety

As discussed in Part 3, psychological safety is where employees at any level feel they can challenge the status quo without negative consequences. In my leadership programs I talk about what people fear most in demonstrating real leadership in their respective teams and organisations. There are many common elements, and interestingly, it doesn't matter at what level of the organisation we listen, we hear much the same fears:

'I'll lose my job.'

'My performance review (and, therefore, my remuneration and/or incentives) may be negatively affected.'

'My boss will make life difficult for me.' (including CEOs who believe this).

'People won't like me.'

'I'll be branded a troublemaker.'

Creating high levels of trust and safety are, therefore, critical.

Create and Regulate Disequilibrium

A key part of a leader's role is to create and regulate distress. Adaptive work generates distress, but there should be a balance between people being in 'sleep mode', and feeling so *distressed* that they become non-productive and wracked with fear and a sense of self-preservation. Heifetz, Grashow and Linsky call it *productive disequilibrium,* where people feel the heat of change but are still able to function well to make progress on the challenge before them. They recommend leaders attend to three fundamental tasks in order to help maintain a productive level of tension:

1. Create what can be called a holding environment (like a pressure cooker, where the heat and pressure are regulated).

2. Be responsible for direction, protection, orientation, managing conflict, and shaping norms.

3. Maintain presence and poise (regulating distress is perhaps a leader's most difficult job).

If You're Going to Manage Anyone, Manage Yourself

In modern organisations, where sometimes progress is rewarded at any cost, internal competition is high, political game-playing is the norm, and people feel the need to engage in self-protective behaviours (for example, passive-aggressive or passive-defensive behaviours), being oneself can be a challenge. Remaining open and authentic, however, is critical in the workplace, whether or not you are a formal leader.

This is a view shared by many researchers and writers. Dee Hock, for example, says that the 'first and paramount responsibility of anyone who purports to manage is to manage self: one's own integrity, character, ethics, knowledge, wisdom, temperament, words, and acts (Hock, 1999). We spend little time and rarely excel at management of self, precisely because it is so much more difficult than prescribing and controlling the behaviour of others. Hock continues to say, however, that without management of self, no one is fit for authority, no matter how much they acquire; for the more authority they acquire the more dangerous they become.

This is about saying what is really on our minds, sharing our fears and concerns at the appropriate time, and not pretending to be something we're not. It can be enormously liberating, particularly in teams, when the team moves to a whole new level of realness. I've seen huge gains in cooperation, trust, communication and, importantly, performance.

There is no doubt that changing paradigms is very difficult. To move to a new paradigm, we must *let go of antiquated models* that do not serve us in the 21st century. It means moving from authority-based management and behaviours to shared leadership. Hock says,

> The problem is that nothing else is going to work. We have tried all the easy ways – the one-minute leader, situational, contingency, great person, nice guy/tough guy trait approaches – and they don't work. So maybe it is time to get serious and try the difficult but more promising approach. It is time to move from an understanding of leadership centered on the individual to one centered on a relationship (Hock, 1999).

Nothing I am proposing changes the nature of accountability. Those in formal authority positions need to maintain 100 per cent accountability for the actions and decisions of people who report to them in some way. Paradoxically, *giving away control by increasing autonomy increases accountability* as people need to think more independently and make decisions accordingly.

Summary

Effective leadership requires a number of often under-developed skills. One of the most important considerations is being able to develop systems intelligence—or an ability to see the whole system, including patterns and interdependencies.

Giving the 'work' back to the people who have the problem is at the heart of leading adaptively and empowering people to make sustainable change.

Whistle-blowers, creative deviants and those who call attention to things other people would rather ignore are routinely smashed and silenced in organisations. We must learn to protect minority voices.

Psychological safety is where employees, at any level, feel they can challenge the status quo without negative consequences. Leaders need to be able to create an environment where psychological safety is present for all employees.

A key part of a leader's role is to create and regulate distress. Adaptive work generates distress, but there should be a balance between people being in 'sleep mode', and feeling so distressed that they become non-productive and wracked with fear and a sense of self-preservation.

If you're going to manage anyone, manage yourself. In modern organisations, where sometimes progress is rewarded at any cost, being oneself can be a challenge. How we deploy ourselves in service of organisational objectives should be carefully considered and constantly adapted. Remaining open and authentic, however, is critical in the workplace, whether or not you are a formal leader.

CHAPTER 11

INFLUENCING WITHOUT AUTHORITY

It is an illusion that once upon a time managers could make their direct reports do whatever was needed. Nobody has ever had enough authority—they never have, and never will. Organizational life is too complicated for that.
—Allan R. Cohen

A Critical Skill for the 21st Century

Such is the demand for us to speak, consult and coach on 'influencing without authority', that a whole chapter has been dedicated to this topic. It seems that in modern organisations, the ability to get people to do what you want them to do, in service of a greater goal or objective, isn't as easy as it used to be.

Perhaps we have become more sensitive to the exercise of authority as we seek greater levels of autonomy and empowerment? Or perhaps organisations have become more complex in how they operate, moving away from the traditional 'up and down the line' hierarchical structures to something more organic? For example, one of the diagnostic tools we utilise is a network analysis, where we take people through a process that helps them understand the formal and informal structures, relationships, and politics in a deeper way. It's like having an organisational x-ray, enabling leaders to see challenges and opportunities in a new or different way.

Whatever the reason, the ability to influence individuals, teams and business units has become a critical skill to be able to get things done. No longer can we rely on the authority vested in our formal job descriptions. While important, it is simply not enough. We must become smarter in how we go about engaging with people with whom we need to collaborate, need something from, or need them to embrace change or support us in our endeavours.

According to Dan Pink, author of *To Sell is Human* (Pink, 2013) to be successful at your job, you must be able to:

1. Sell an idea or project.

2. Persuade coworkers or peers to provide support and/or resources, or

3. Get people to do something that they may not necessarily want or need to do.

In fact, Pink's analysis showed that about 70 per cent of roles involve 'selling', so whether you know it – or like it – you *are in* sales.

Understanding Authority

We have talked about authority and the differences between it and leadership. The reality is, however, that for many of our influencing challenges, we do not have any formal authority 'over' the key people involved. We can think about formal authority as that vested in our role (through a job description, for example) – whether that be a permanent team, a team brought together for a specific purpose, or purely based on our position in the hierarchy. Informal authority, on the other hand, is entirely in the eyes of the observer. In a general sense, informal authority can be enhanced by investing in building high-trust relationships, being credible, and being seen to behave in a values-driven way.

We can think about informal authority like our 'currency' or 'what we have to offer' in the eyes of others. And it changes – for example, with one stakeholder you might have a high currency around your technical knowledge, while with another it could be your ability to build relationships. You may know people in your organisation who don't necessarily hold senior positions, but people listen when they talk because they possess a certain currency that the organisation values.

So the bottom line is to understand your authority and currency within the system.

The Role of Trust

The 'trust formula' (Maister, et al., 2001) is a useful way to think about informal authority. The key elements to be enhanced include credibility, reliability and intimacy. The area we need to decrease is self-orientation. Table 4 describes each area in more detail. If you were to think about the levels of trust present in your work relationships, where would you be strong? Where might you be weak? Importantly, it is other people's assessment of the trust between us that is also important.

Being able to think about - and invest time in - the four elements of trust may seem like a slower pathway than other methods. However, your efforts will be rewarded many times over. Also, the four elements shouldn't be thought of as just a 'destination' or 'endpoint'. We should aim to engage with others in accordance with the four elements *in everything we do,* right from the first meeting. A lot has been written about how quickly others assess our likeability and trustworthiness – it's much quicker than we think, or perhaps would like it to be. If we can consistently demonstrate and build credibility, reliability and intimacy together with low levels of self-orientation, then our ability to influence others will be amplified.

COMPONENT	REALM	EXAMPLE
Credibility	Words	I can trust what he/she says about...
Reliability	Actions	I can trust he/she to...
Intimacy	Emotions	I feel comfortable discussing...
Self-orientation	Motives	I can trust that he/she cares about...

Table 4: Key elements of trust to build informal authority and influencing firepower (Maister, Green and Galford).

Influencing People Just to Get Something Doesn't Cut It Anymore

Leadership without influencing isn't leadership. But how we do it is critical in today's context. Considering all that has been written about how to influence people, I couldn't help think that some influencing frameworks were incomplete, too narrowly focused, or in some cases, relied too heavily on the idea of exchange. This view is too simplistic and may in fact create a transactional mindset – 'I've got something you value, so let's do business!' This is only part of what we need to think about.

Engagement Model

From working with leaders and teams for over two decades, I have discovered what works and what doesn't work in terms of influencing other people. To bring that thinking together, I have created an engagement model to guide thinking and action. The key elements of an engagement model should help us:

1. Be clear about what we want.

2. Understand the present context (being politically savvy).

3. Identify the right people you need to influence, and who can help along the way.

4. Create a clear plan of action.

5. Create engagement.

The Engagement Model below incorporates the key aspects of influencing. While the model doesn't encompass *all* aspects of creating an influencing strategy, it focusses on the areas where leaders seem to encounter the most challenges.

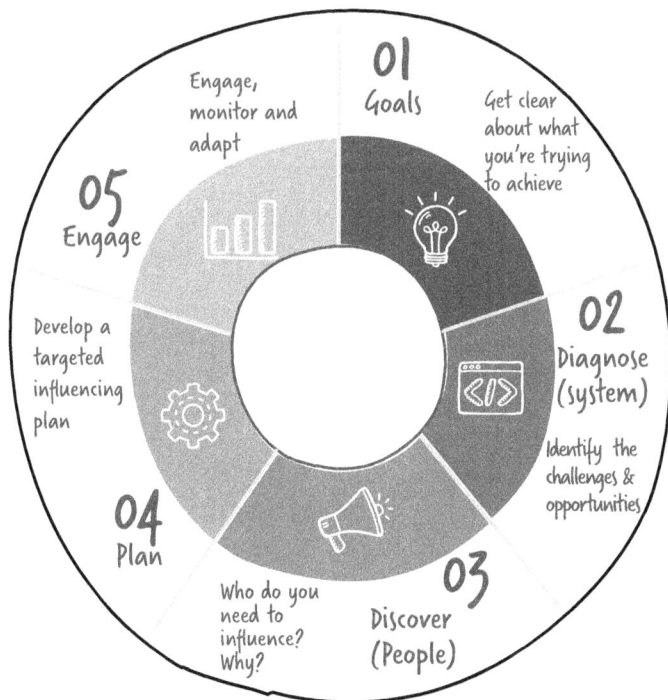

Figure 15: Influencing Engagement Model

What Should I Be Focusing On?

The model can be thought of in three parts:

1. Understand (Goals, Diagnose and Discover).
2. Guide (Plan).
3. Act (Engage).

Understand

It ensures, first and foremost, that we truly understand the context in which we operate. My experience is that it doesn't matter how senior or experienced managers are, one or more steps are usually missed with predictable negative outcomes. As discussed earlier, step 2 is critical in being able to understand the difference between adaptive and technical elements, and then formulating a suitable intervention.

By reflecting and seeking to answer three questions in each of the five areas, we can save ourselves a lot of heartache, pain, frustration and re-work.

Engagement Model: Influencing Without Authority		
PHASE	WHAT'S IT ABOUT?	WHAT QUESTIONS SHOULD I ASK?
1. Goal	Your goal or framing should be strong enough to spark interest	1. What is my goal? 2. What value will be created if I'm successful? For me? For the organisation? 3. How should I frame the challenge or opportunity?
2. Diagnose (system)	Identify the challenges and opportunities by seeing the whole system and how it interacts.	4. How might I look at the challenge through different eyes? 5. As part of the system, what have I 'caused'? 6. How much heat is there? How much should there be to advance the cause?

3. Discover (people)	Identify who you need to influence and why.	7. Who has power and interest in the initiative? 8. What level of trust and currency (something they value) do I have with each? 9. What are their triggers (threat/reward)?
4. Plan	Develop a targeted influencing and change plan.	10. How do I continue to make progress and build momentum? 11. What are the bold and small steps I need to take? 12. Who can support me to implement my plan?
5. Engage	Engage with key people, monitor the response and adapt accordingly.	13. How do I find common ground to proceed? 14. How do I best engage with individuals and groups? 15. How do I continually learn and adapt my approach?

Table 5: Engagement model in detail

Guide

The Engagement Model serves as a guide to ensure that all critical aspects of influencing people are considered. It avoids the awkward interactions where neither party is particularly clear on 'what's on the table' or what the respective agendas might be.

Act

Finally, the model helps ensure that our actions are going to make a difference. Because influencing and change are inter-connected, many of the same traps are present. How we act and engage key people in the conversations that matter will largely determine the outcomes. People watch us very closely to see how we engage with others (particularly when loss is involved), to determine how they will engage with us when it counts.

(Please visit the free tools section at www.theleadershipsphere. com.au for a roadmap that will help you formulate an effective plan).

Are You the One Getting in the Way?

It is worth reinforcing one of the questions in the diagnose phase: 'As part of the system, what have I caused?'

You are no doubt passionate about your project, initiative or crusade. But don't let your love for your initiative get in the way of your effectiveness. It is common for people to become overly-invested to the point they can't see another way forward. We need to have the presence of mind to 'zoom out' (look at the bigger picture), take a breath and reflect on how we are complicit in the current state – the good, the bad and the ugly.

Only when you're able to engage in a more neutral way and talk about the collective benefits, will your influencing strategy truly take flight.

Summary

Influencing others when we don't have authority has become a critical skill.

An analysis of job roles indicates that up to 70 per cent involve 'selling' in some way, meaning that for many, you are in 'sales'.

To be able to influence effectively, it is helpful to understand the role of authority and trust.

Our Influencing Engagement Model helps to understand influencing in three key areas:

1. Understand.

2. Guide.

3. Act.

It also outlines five important steps:

1. Goals.

2. Diagnose (system).

3. Discover (people).

4. Plan.

5. Engage.

One of the most important considerations is YOU and the role you have played so far in the challenge or opportunity.

PART 5:

THE SEVEN SPHERES
OF LEADERSHIP
MASTERY IN
PRACTICE

CHAPTER 12

MANAGE AND LEAD CHANGE

Two-thirds of all change initiatives fail. This is a sobering fact for all managers and leaders in organisations. Senior executive Robert Dale from Asia Pacific Inc.[1] needed to change the organisation's culture to meet the needs of the newly-developed strategy. He needed everyone in the organisation – not just those in formal leadership positions – to be engaged in the change process, actively working to reduce inefficient processes, and address poor customer service and the subsequent below-par financial results.

On the surface, and according to most management texts, Robert did everything right. He knew that he had to create a compelling story, because employees must see the point of the change and agree with it.

Robert discussed the need to role model the new behaviours with his executive team and the need to align reinforcement mechanisms such as systems, processes, and incentives. Robert consulted with his HR department to ensure that relevant development programs were put in place to build capability so employees would have the skills required to make the desired changes.

After 12 months' worth of time, energy and money, the change outcomes remained patchy and isolated. The strategy also remained a theoretical framework for change. Customer service remained low, and in some cases there was evidence that employees were actively resisting the change. By any measure, the change had

---

1   Robert and Asia Pacific Inc. are pseudonyms. However, Robert is a composite of real leaders.

failed and the organisation was now vulnerable to competitive forces.

So what went wrong? There were a number of fatal errors. Robert had failed to take into account contemporary insights about human nature – insights that if not carefully considered would get in the way of applying the necessary conditions required for meaningful, positive change.

First, what often motivates you doesn't motivate your employees. What the leader cares about (and typically bases at least 80 per cent of his or her message to others on) does not tap into roughly 80 per cent of the workforce's primary motivators for putting extra energy into the change program.

Well-intentioned leaders invest significant time in communicating their change story. While this is necessary, more time should be invested in listening, not telling, and involving employees in the conversation about the change. We also know that many leaders focus their story on the deficit approach or the burning platform. There are a couple of potential problems with this approach. First, when the platform is no longer 'burning', for example, it is only 'luke warm': what is the imperative for change? Second, while the burning platform metaphor may appeal to some employees, many are looking for a positive reason to change, for example, what the organisation is trying to create. We could call this the 'burning ambition'.

In terms of role-modelling appropriate behaviours, leaders believe mistakenly that they already 'are the change'. Robert believed he had built a high-trust environment. However, his mixed messages to different executives, effectively 'playing them off against each other' destroyed trust. The ripple effect was felt throughout the entire organisation.

Executives often commit to role modelling constructive behaviours – and then, in practice, nothing significant changes. The reason for this is that most executives don't count themselves among the ones who need to change. How many executives would answer 'no' to the question 'Are you a team-player?', and 'yes' to the question 'Are you a blocker?' The answer is none. The fact is that human beings consistently think they are better than they are, and that others are worse than they actually are. We judge ourselves by our intentions and others by their actions.

Robert also failed to adequately motivate and energise people around the change. There are also many myths about reinforcing mechanisms and what motivates people. For example, money is the most expensive motivator, while small, unexpected rewards can pay for themselves many times over. Any change also needs to be perceived as fair. Reality doesn't actually matter, it's what employees think that matters.

Many of the problems Robert faced were systemic and adaptive – that is, those without a defined solution that required fundamental changes in values, beliefs, priorities and loyalties. Legitimate, yet competing perspectives emerged and Robert's formal leaders were not adequately prepared or skilled to deal with them effectively. They were used to applying quick technical fixes to issues that needed to be explored more deeply so that meaningful progress could be made.

To effectively lead change in this environment, leaders need a particular approach and skillset. Skills include systems intelligence, the ability to actually identify the adaptive component of their various challenges, being able to turn the heat up and down as required, and maintaining disciplined attention on the change process. Robert's leaders failed on almost every count because they were used to operating from an old 'command and control', linear doctrine.

To avoid being one of the two-thirds of projects that fail, adopt positive change. This requires letting go of old patterns and taking a fresh perspective. It includes a focus on opportunities rather than problems, long-term versus short-term thinking, and building adaptability versus controlling people and things.

Summary

Two-thirds of all change initiatives fail. This is a sobering fact for all managers and leaders in organisations. Despite having the right intentions, managers often fail to create meaningful, long-term change, with results often being patchy.

Managers can fall into familiar traps, such as not understanding insights about human nature, not engaging people in a conversation about change, focusing too heavily or narrowly on a 'burning platform' story, and believing that they have built and created a high trust environment.

Managers, in fact people in general, often believe they are demonstrating appropriate and constructive behaviours yet grossly underestimate the need for the change required in themselves.

Managers often misdiagnose and underestimate the systemic and adaptive nature of organisational challenges and opportunities. Specifically, addressing the changes required in values, beliefs, priorities and loyalties. Technical solutions are often applied where an adaptive approach is demanded.

CHAPTER 13

ACTION-ORIENTED

In an attempt to catch up to competitors, Asia Pacific Inc. needed new growth. The strategy needed to allow API to improve its innovation capability and get crucial products and services to market quicker than its competitors.

Robert instructed his executive team to formulate project teams that would allow API to review its business practices, policies, procedures, and culture to support the new strategy. Three project teams were formulated, each headed by one of the three division heads. After six months, it was clear that each of the teams was burning money and using valuable resources. Progress was negligible, and in some cases, problems rather than solutions had been encountered.

Taking the wrong action in organisations is endemic – and the evidence is overwhelming. A study conducted by John Kotter in 1996, and more recent research conducted by McKinsey, show that seven out of ten change efforts fail. How can this be so? More importantly, how much money is mismanagement of change costing your organisation? The figure may well frighten you, but as a rough estimate, calculate the cost of everyone in your company who is working on changing behaviours, systems, processes or structures and then assume that 70 per cent of that figure is money down the drain. No organisation can afford this; it is costing you dearly.

So what went wrong with the three project teams appointed by Robert? The problem literally started at the top. While a growth strategy had been formulated, it was a poor plan put together by Robert and one member of the team (who had 'strategy' as part of their portfolio). The document had been discussed three times by the entire executive team, with each discussion lasting a couple of hours. While Robert believed that executive team members were provided ample opportunities to debate the strategy and provide input, the reality, in the team's mind, was very different. As I have seen dozens of times, most members of the executive team did not feel they debated the pros and cons of the strategy at all. In fact, half the team thought it was the wrong strategy altogether, but failed to speak up strongly enough to be heard.

So why didn't seasoned executives speak up and challenge Robert and each other? They simply didn't feel safe to do so. In the back of their minds, they remember the executive who was asked to leave last year, who, in their view, was the only one who challenged Robert regularly. Whether this is the real reason he was asked to leave doesn't matter—perception is reality. Because executive team members didn't have 'buy in' to the strategy (at best) and disagreed and even undermined the strategy (at worst), the project teams were actually *impotent*. Despite his good intentions, Robert had provided *counterfeit* and *myopic leadership* by expecting project teams to come up with the answers when he, as the CEO, hadn't laid a solid foundation. The resulting entropy caused the organisation to *increase* the rate of deterioration, rather than *arrest* it.

Other initiatives were also largely impotent. The culture change project hinged on a diagnosis done internally by people with an overly-simplistic understanding of culture. The diagnosis was flawed in its design and failed to uncover key legacy issues. Other examples of downright destructive actions included poorly-managed restructures (used as a Band-Aid and not addressing the intended issues); trotting out familiar training programs that didn't challenge the status quo; defining the challenge to fit the current expertise; and simply denying that some of the key problems within Asia Pacific Inc. actually existed.

What could Robert have done differently? Robert *and* his executive team needed to role-model the aspirational culture by encouraging and having crucial conversations, building trust and listening to the challenges people faced at all levels of the organisation. There is no doubt that Robert could have helped people face reality as it related to their condition, threats and opportunities. He needed to effectively *mobilise* the organisation to do adaptive work and adjust their values, habits, practices and priorities. Real leaders take responsibility for being the source of the movement, rather than waiting for other people.

At an individual level, it is about creating a safe environment to enable others to fulfil their potential—to be their best. It's about coaching others rather than trying to control them, drawing out talents and strengths in the service of team and organisational objectives. Leaders need to have high levels of self-awareness, and the ability to *create tension* at the right time and with the right people to overcome *inertia*.

Also, had Robert supported the change agenda with *team and individual coaching,* he would have found that people and teams would have taken responsibility for change at all levels of the organisation. People would have been more accepting of new information, demonstrated higher levels of commitment to change and then taken definitive and stepwise action towards the goal.

People would have been energised and focused on creating a company that was 'fit-for-purpose' for the strategic objectives. There would have been no wasted energy on activities and tasks that kept everybody busy but didn't really achieve much. *To do anything else is a costly and largely futile exercise.*

Summary

While there is generally a bias for action in organisations, the actions taken must be appropriate in order to make progress.

If 70 per cent of all change fails to deliver the intended benefits, the cost to companies can be huge. As an approximate estimate, calculate the cost of everyone in your company who is working on changing behaviours, systems, processes or structures and then assume that 70 per cent of that figure is money down the drain.

Managers often fail to engage colleagues sufficiently well, sometimes believing that knowledge equals understanding and support.

Counterfeit and myopic leadership can result from misdiagnosis and a poor understanding of people.

Psychological safety is an essential element in creating and sustaining a high performing team and organisation.

Managers need to role-model the aspirational culture by encouraging and having crucial conversations, building trust and listening to the challenges people face at all levels of the organisation. It's about coaching others to create commitment rather than trying to control them.

CHAPTER 14

SYNERGY

Synergy simply means that the effect of the whole is greater than the sum of the effects of the individual parts. In undertaking any initiative, particularly formulating strategy and building a 'fit-for-purpose' and values-based culture, creating synergy is a must-have. Synergy, in an organisational sense, means building relationships, enabling a collaborative environment, creating constructive conflict to tease out people's real views, and managing and leading teams effectively.

Robert and the executive team demonstrated poor skills in helping to provide an environment based on real relationships. Robert was 'old school' in fostering competition among his team members, falsely believing it created higher levels of performance. This competition created a silo mentality between key divisions and ultimately led to lower levels of overall performance.

The culture at API was also very command and control-oriented, where people were expected to comply with managerial expectations without making a fuss. This translated into a toxic culture of high avoidance and compliance; passivity, approval-seeking, and aggressive behaviours. One of the cultural norms that existed within the organisation was that managers were the 'boss' because they had more experience and, therefore, knew the right actions to take. Many managers within API, including CEO Robert, prided themselves on being no-nonsense leaders. They were often hard on their people to get results, a practice that was overlooked most of the time because they 'met their numbers'.

The story within the organisation was that 'until someone tells me I should behave differently, I'll continue to manage how I choose'.

Numbers-driven leaders are often seen as results-driven and good for business, but they are hardly *ever* good for business in the medium to long term. *They effectively burn people.* They fail to balance the pragmatic and necessary focus on results with the necessary second face or dimension—people. It is a cliché to say that people are an organisation's most important resource, but even this statement misses the point, because people *are* your organisation, not just a resource!

Just because the CEO didn't seem to have a problem with a 'no-nonsense' numbers-driven leadership style, didn't mean *it* wasn't a problem; there was indeed a cost. Many people *hated* working there and employee turnover was higher than in most of its peer organisations. Many talented people only stayed for a short period, and it had always been hard to attract good people to the company. Engagement scores had also just about bottomed out, indicating some serious problems.

Effective leaders, or true leaders, are able to build relationships and high-performance teams in the service of organisational goals, not despite them. *Long-term sustainable performance requires people at all levels of the organisation to be engaged and focused on the job at hand.* They need to feel their opinion counts; that they have a say in how things are run, and that the organisation has their interests at heart.

People need to be able to feel the values and good intentions of those in formal positions of authority. Employees need to know (and see) leaders serving those in the organisation who actually do the work—usually those closest to the customer. Senior leaders exist to make others more successful, not the other way around!

Two key attributes of effective leaders are emotional intelligence and presence. Emotionally intelligent leadership would dictate that Robert and senior managers (as a minimum) at Asia Pacific Inc. demonstrate empathy, self-awareness, and the ability to manage their own emotions and control their responses, particularly when feeling threatened or when under stress. Presence, on the other hand, is the ability to be completely present and fully attend to those around you. A practical example of not being present is when people continue typing while talking to others, fiddle with their phones while pretending to listen, or simply think about something else unrelated to the conversation. Being fully present can be wonderfully inspirational, and rapidly build credibility and relationships.

Leaders like Robert and his team need to understand that leadership is not an individualistic exercise, but rather a shared and co-created one. They need to put their egos aside at times, and let others 'step up' and lead, particularly those in the best positions to voice a view based on where and what they do, not their formal position in the hierarchy. This may mean, for example, that a graduate may have more answers than the CEO in some circumstances.

To create synergy, leaders need to surface and manage conflict constructively, and create safety for people to talk about the real issues. Leaders need to manage both 'cool' and 'hot' topics within the team. Cool topics have more certainty, more available data and, therefore, usually lower levels of emotion. Hot topics, on the other hand, can be characterised by being more subjective, often with no readily available answers (for example, adaptive challenges). They are hard to test, have higher levels of emotion and disagreement and often get 'personal'.

Paradoxically, effective leaders sometimes need to provoke the system, for example, a team to overcome inertia. Consider a much-vaunted former leader of GE, Jack Welch, who talked about how, when he first arrived at GE, his new management team had an air of 'superficial congeniality'. In other words, it was an ineffective team that thought being nice to each other was being a high-performance team. To provoke the system, Jack used to throw 'hand grenades', metaphorically speaking of course, to surface the real issues.

So, in summary, effective leaders must demonstrate competencies in both interpersonal skills as well as a focus on results. They must have high levels of self-awareness, as well as being able to read situations, and other people, well. They must use their own emotions in an intelligent way. They must be authentic and demonstrate core personal and organisational values, not just talk about them. Leaders like Robert must build and maintain relationships with factions or groups with different interests and agendas to their own. This is the work of real leadership.

Summary

In undertaking any initiative, particularly formulating strategy and building a 'fit-for-purpose' and values-based culture, creating synergy is a must-have. Synergy, in an organisational sense, means building relationships, enabling a collaborative environment, creating constructive conflict to tease out people's real views, and managing and leading teams effectively.

Too often in today's organisations, senior leaders create an environment that fosters unhealthy competition and a silo mentality, ultimately leading to lower levels of performance.

A command and control culture can create a toxic culture of high avoidance and compliance; passivity, approval-seeking, and aggressive behaviours.

The sole measure of success should not, and cannot be simply 'meeting their numbers'. Numbers-driven leaders are often seen as results-driven and good for business, but they are hardly ever good for business in the medium to long term.

Effective leaders, or true leaders, are able to build relationships and high-performance teams in the service of organisational goals, not despite them. Long-term sustainable performance requires people at all levels of the organisation to be engaged and focused on the job at hand.

Two key attributes of effective leaders are emotional intelligence and presence.

Leaders need to understand that leadership is not an individualistic exercise, but rather a shared and co-created one. Leaders need to surface and manage conflict constructively, and create safety for people to talk about the real issues.

Leaders must build and maintain relationships with factions or groups with different interests and agendas to their own. This is the work of real leadership.

CHAPTER 15

TRUTH

Children know a lot about leadership. They have a gift for telling it as it is; in effect, expressing what they're thinking and feeling. My children, for example, don't mind telling me that they don't like what I'm wearing, or that when I say something they don't agree with that 'I'm just being silly'.

Truth and authenticity are sadly often missing in leadership. Yet when it is demonstrated, people connect with the leader in unexpected ways. Let's return to Robert, our hapless CEO whose organisation, API, needs to formulate and execute a new strategy just to keep up with its competitors. So far, little progress has been made in surfacing the real issues where progress needs to be made, or in building a constructive culture to serve the strategy.

Robert had (on the surface, at least) done a number of things right, for example, his road shows. However, the way he went about selling his vision was flawed. Robert was not driven by a strong sense of purpose around the strategy or the organisation, and this came through during his presentations. They were largely lifeless, data-heavy slideshows that failed to engage people in the most fundamental of ways—at the levels of head, heart, hands and spirit (purposefulness). The 'killer blow' for Robert was that he failed to speak the truth and tell it 'as it was'. Instead, he made a number of references to external factors and how difficult it had been for him and the executive. At no time did he take responsibility for their lacklustre performance. Worse still, Robert had not learnt how to be authentic. The art of telling a powerful story can move the most resistant and cynical person, if crafted correctly. When listening to him, people weren't sure whether or not to believe him.

I will share a very simple example which demonstrates the converse of Robert; a story that has stuck with me for a long time. Some years ago I was running a leadership program for a group of 30-something banking employees. They were a mix of marketing professionals, analysts, and managers. I asked the question, 'Who do you find most inspiring as a leader?' Almost all of the group chose a senior woman—let's call her Christine—they met on a recent site visit. It was what Christine did that I found to be the most surprising. During Christine's visit to their interstate office, she spent time walking around and chatting to people, asking them what they did and what were their challenges. Expecting them to finish with a heroic leadership story, they said what they found inspiring was that she cared and took the time to talk to them as people. She was interested in them and showed that their goals were more important than hers.

How do you think her department performed? Exceptionally well. She had a simple yet powerful style. *What you say matters, what you think matters, and I'm here to support you.* This demonstrated that people matter. Upon further investigation, however, she did a lot more. Christine did what children do so well—she was real. In developing and leading her 3,000+ staff, she focused on positive change by constantly reminding people of why they were there and where they were heading. There were no great speeches seeking to enhance her own status and ego. Instead, she focused on simple yet powerful stories about customers who had received service beyond what was expected, and what it meant to them. She sometimes asked customers to meet staff who would normally never come into contact with customers (usually her own senior people). She focused on what was working in the business. She focused on people's strengths rather than weaknesses. Weaknesses were not ignored, but largely extinguished through smart management.

Christine constantly talked about values, her own and the stated organisational values. She backed up this talk through constant demonstration of a commitment to the values. For example, when making decisions in her team, she would foster meaningful (and often tough) conversations about the pros and cons of a decision, taking into consideration the business objectives, shareholders, customers and staff. Values were used as a touchstone for all decisions.

Is this the right thing to do? Indeed. Christine was inspiring leaders to openly communicate their principles and what they stood for despite their popularity. Most importantly, they were learning to model the behaviours required to move towards a high-performance culture. They truly walked the talk in everything they did. Her team had a sense of purpose (and urgency) which was infused throughout her department. People felt engaged in the work that mattered. While everyone worked very hard, they could see beyond themselves and were reminded of the bigger picture. Their contribution was recognised formally and informally on a regular basis.

Christine also understood one key thing: that leadership is about creating leadership in others—not doing it to them. She didn't buy into the 'leader-follower' paradigm, knowing that this can create enormous dependence, inertia and underperformance in organisations. Christine and her management team knew that to achieve their stretch goals consistently, they could not afford to manage and lead in a top-down traditional way.

People need to understand where they are going, and why. It is the job of senior management to help create the conditions that enable people to take ownership and accountability for their results at all levels of the department. This happens in three ways: encouraging people to take action at the local level; providing a culture where it was okay to speak up and challenge; and supporting people to be their best.

Underpinning all of this, however, is a sense of authenticity. People always knew where they stood with Christine. Far from being a wilting flower, she was not afraid to have the tough conversations. The difference was that she did this in a very constructive way. Her leadership team knew it could have real conversations, not those sanitised by the weight of expectation about how a team was meant to have conversations. Conflict was not only managed, it was encouraged. Underlying issues were surfaced and dealt with before they damaged the team. Consequently, trust levels were high and people in the team knew that each member had their eye on the collective, not the individual prize. Christine rewarded this attitude and actively discouraged individualistic behaviour.

Christine's leadership style created an atmosphere of commitment. When a decision was made, the team got right behind it and committed to a plan of action. Even if some people disagreed with the decision, the very fact that they had been heard on the issue allowed them to accept it. They held each other accountable for collective results and didn't tolerate anything less. Conversations were authentic. Christine knew there was no such thing as a dysfunctional team or department, in that each was perfectly aligned to get the results it achieved. Her team were different as they actively worked on aligning the team for achievement and success.

Once Christine and her team were able to positively influence the lives of those around them, they would be engaged in the act of leadership and each of them would, in effect, be creating a legacy. Our leadership legacy is the sum total of the difference we make in people's lives. Many leaders fail to consciously craft their legacy, instead leaving it to chance. Christine knew that she wanted to leave the organisation much stronger and more self-sufficient than when she arrived. By being true to ourselves and the organisational mission, we set up a foundation for success. That brings us back to children and what they can teach us about leadership. While strategy and vision-setting are important, it's only part of the story.

Children can teach us that to be a successful leader we need to be real – real in our relationships, real in how we interact and real about what we think people most need in organisations. Today, people need a more humanistic environment where they can be their best in the service of business goals and an organisational mission they care about. Robert, and many leaders like him, would do well to take a leaf out of Christine's book.

Summary

Children know a lot about leadership. They have a gift for telling it as it is; in effect, expressing what they're thinking and feeling. Often however, truth and authenticity are missing in leadership.

Leaders must have, and demonstrate, a strong sense of purpose and an ability to talk straight with people. Being able to tell a powerful story to contextualise the change can help move people forward.

Leaders who are seen as inspiring are often good at doing the simple things such as spending time walking around talking to people and demonstrating that they matter. They also focus on people's strengths rather than weaknesses.

Effective leaders also understand their personal values and know how to connect them to organisational values. They also back up this talk through a constant demonstration of their commitment to the values.

Leadership is about creating leadership in others—not doing it to them.

It is the job of senior management to help create the conditions that enable people to take ownership and accountability for their results at all levels of the department or organisation. This includes being able to engage in real conversations with people.

Our leadership legacy is the sum total of the difference we make in people's lives. Many leaders fail to consciously craft their legacy, instead leaving it to chance.

Today, people need a more humanistic environment where they can be their best in the service of business goals and an organisational mission they care about.

CHAPTER 16

ENGAGE

Leaders need to create a compelling vision or picture of the future that promotes a highly-focused, results-driven culture. Robert failed to engage his own team or organisation. While most leaders love to make strategy, it's vision and values that can doom a strategy. An organisation's vision needs to energise people; it needs to be more than a 'let's-go-through-the-motions' type statement.

A true vision shapes all activities, including recruitment and selection, reward and recognition, and how customers, shareholders and suppliers are treated. In today's chaotic world, and aligned to the principles of adaptive leadership, leaders should also be encouraged to adopt a more experimental approach to strategic planning, running multiple micro-strategies and then adapting resource allocation according to effectiveness.

Team Charter Canvass

I developed a framework that helps leaders think about how to engage their people (Figure 16). The order of why, how, and what, borrows from Simon Sinek's work and helps ensure we focus on the 'why' first and foremost. This is different to how many leaders think and communicate, often starting with the 'what' and the 'how', and neglecting the 'why' (Sinek, 2011). This framework can be used as a simple diagnostic, by asking team members to rate each element (1 to 10) and then discuss their ratings.

Organisational vision and mission

In simple terms, it asks the team to think about the organisational vision and mission first, to ensure there is clarity. If there is not, then the clarity needs to be established either through creating it, or seeking clarification from the top team.

Team vision, mission and contribution

Once there is clarity about the organisational mission and vision, only then will a team be in a position to identify its own vision, mission and the contribution it needs to make to the strategy.

Scope

Team scope seeks to identify the limits of authority, chosen areas of influence, and shared responsibilities. It seeks to answer, *What is in/out of scope?*

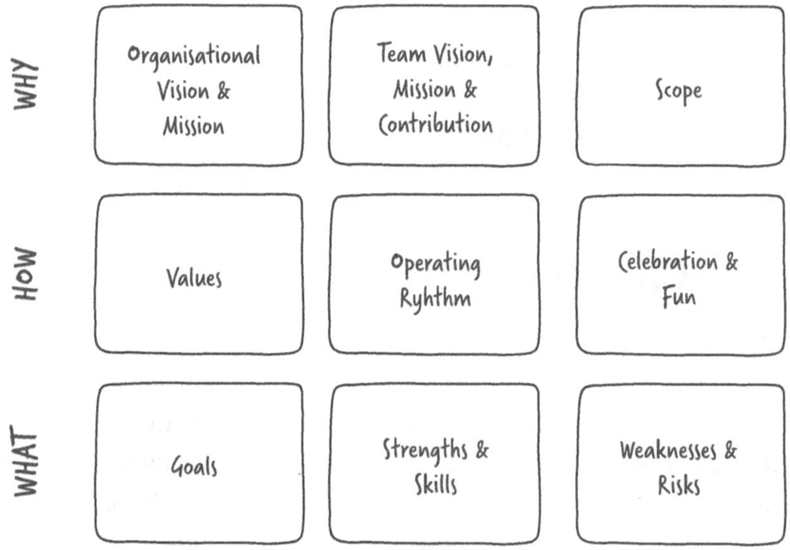

Figure 16: Team charter canvass

Values

Now that the team is clear about the 'why', the focus needs to be on 'how' they will travel together. The question to be asked here is 'How should we behave?' For example, how team members should treat each other, what do effective relationships look like, and how we hold each other accountable around our values.

Operating Rhythm

The key question here is *How* should we work together? This looks at areas such as decision-making; communication; managing conflict; meeting frequency, agenda and rules; and support mechanisms.

Celebration and Fun

How do we celebrate successes and failures and have fun along the way? Key areas to be discussed here include acknowledging each other, fun events, team and relationship building.

Goals

This dimension asks *What* are the measurable team outcomes and performance standards? Rather than a long shopping list of goals and actions—a near fatal affliction—focus on 3–4 Critical Success Factors with a particular focus on exemplary execution.

Strengths and Skills

Once the team is clear on goals, it needs to identify the strengths and skills needed to pull it off. This includes identifying what the team is good at collectively and individually (task and relationship).

Weaknesses and Risks

What skills, collectively and individually, are lacking in the team? What risks need to be managed? What will hinder the team?

In combination, the canvass can be a powerful vehicle to engage team members to help achieve high levels of performance, engagement and sustainability.

(A more comprehensive version is available at www.leadershipsphere.com.au)

So, back to Robert.

He and his executive team failed to engage in robust debate about the best way forward; therefore, didn't formulate or articulate a coherent strategy to accomplish this.

One of the interesting peculiarities about engaging people in change and implementation of strategy is that we often know what needs to be done, but we don't actually do it. Often the rewards for changing are far into the future, while the discomfort, disequilibrium and pain have to be dealt with now. Leaders like Robert, therefore, have to guide, encourage, support and manage the disequilibrium over the short and medium term.

In terms of values, companies with strong values are often more successful. In high-performing companies, values guide behaviour and decision-making. Those who don't behave in accord with organisational values need to receive remedial development and ultimately be asked to leave the organisation (if there is not sufficient improvement). As Jack Welch says, 'you must be public about the consequences of breaching core values. When you announce simply that an executive has "left to pursue other business interests," you lose the chance to make a statement about values.'

Robert needed to employ a disciplined approach to Asia Pacific Inc.'s vision and values. Then guide everyone in the organisation about what needs to be delivered, how it needs to be delivered, and why. One international company I worked with assessed every manager according to two criteria: their current performance and their values. This company used a nine-cell matrix with performance on one axis and values on the other. In a general sense, those who lived the values but whose performance was not up to scratch, were given intensive support to improve. Conversely, high performers whose behaviours did not meet the standards demanded by the values, were also given intensive support; however, if they didn't improve their behaviours, they were asked to leave or were terminated.

A key leadership skill is to influence others. When done well, telling the story about a compelling mission, vision and values can energise an entire organisation. Storytelling can take many shapes, from water-cooler conversations, to personal stories, to large-scale town hall type addresses.

According to Craig Wortmann (Wortmann, 2006), stories:

- Create leadership presence.
- Create a context for listeners.
- Build relationships.
- Illustrate success and failure.
- Allow reflection.
- Act as an antidote from data and information overload.
- Show us the why, how and what.
- Show multiple perspectives.
- Help us unlearn bad habits and behaviours.
- Spread beyond their immediate audiences.

I have found that many leaders lack the self-confidence and know-how to tell powerful, effective stories. However, with a relatively small amount of training, combined with some simple processes to gain clarity about the vision, mission and values, leaders become very excited at being able to tell a great business-related story. After only a small amount of coaching, a CEO I was working with changed his approach and style substantially regarding a major announcement, with excellent outcomes.

Summary

Leaders need to create a compelling vision or picture of the future that promotes a highly-focused, results-driven culture. An organisation's vision needs to energise people; it needs to be more than a 'let's-go-through-the-motions' type statement.

Leaders should also be encouraged to adopt a more experimental approach to strategic planning, running multiple micro-strategies and then adapting resource allocation according to effectiveness.

A useful development framework to engage and develop teams includes nine key areas:

- Organisational vision and mission.
- Team vision, mission and contribution.
- Scope.
- Values.
- Operating rhythm.
- Celebration and fun.
- Goals.
- Strengths and skills.

One of the interesting peculiarities about engaging people in change and implementation of strategy is that we often know what needs to be done, but we don't actually do it. Often the rewards for changing are far into the future, while the discomfort, disequilibrium and pain have to be dealt with now.

In terms of values, companies with strong values are often more successful. In high-performing companies, values guide behaviour and decision-making.

Many leaders lack the self-confidence and know-how to tell powerful, effective stories.

CHAPTER 17

RESILIENCE

After a year of spinning the wheels at API, Robert was feeling despondent. His revitalisation of API was a dismal failure, slipping farther behind the competition with levels of engagement across the organisation at an all-time low.

After working extremely hard over a number of years, combined with the poor shape of API, he was starting to think that perhaps it all wasn't worth it. He began to ask the hard questions about his working life—actually, his life generally. He had risen to CEO of API at a relatively young age, but his sense of enjoyment and fulfilment for his work had all but disappeared. He wasn't sleeping well, often waking in the middle of the night thinking about his 'to do' list. He was eating poorly and was 10 kilograms overweight. He was snappy with people around him, including his family. He pronounced, 'Why can't they understand how much pressure I'm under?'

Does any of this sound or feel familiar? Can you see some of yourself in Robert? We live in a global village connected by digital media. Our pace is rushed, rapid-fire, and relentless. Facing crushing workloads, we try to cram as much as possible into every day. Time management is no longer a viable solution. We need more. It's not about 'coping' or 'surviving'; it's a state of mind which is not helpful. We shouldn't just 'get by', it's not fair to our work colleagues or the organisation, and it's not fair to our family and friends. Most importantly, however, you deserve more.

'Resilience is the process of adapting well in the face of adversity, trauma, tragedy, threats, or even significant sources of stress – such as family and relationship problems, serious health problems, or workplace and financial stressors. It means "bouncing back" from difficult experiences.' (American Psychological Society, 2010)

Resilience is not a trait that people either have or do not have. It involves behaviours, thoughts, and actions that can be learned and developed in anyone. A combination of factors contributes to resilience:

- Caring and supportive relationships.
- The capacity to make realistic plans and take steps to carry them out.
- A positive view of yourself, and confidence in your strengths and abilities.
- Skills in communication and problem-solving.
- The capacity to manage strong feelings and impulses.

All of these are factors that people can develop in themselves. Robert could consider the following strategies to build resilience (American Psychological Society, 2010):

1. Making connections. Good relationships with close family members, friends, or others are important.

2. Avoiding seeing crises as insurmountable problems. You can't change the fact that highly stressful events happen, but you can change how you interpret and respond to these events.

3. Accepting that change is a part of living.

4. Moving toward your goals. Develop some realistic goals. Do something regularly (even if it seems like a small accomplishment) that moves you toward your goals.

5. Taking decisive actions. Act on adverse situations as much as you can. Take decisive actions, rather than detaching completely from problems and stresses and wishing they would just go away.

6. Looking for opportunities for self-discovery. People often learn something about themselves, and may find that they have grown in some respect as a result of their struggle with loss.

7. Nurturing a positive view of yourself. Developing confidence in your ability to solve problems and trusting your instincts helps build resilience.

8. Keeping things in perspective. Even when facing very painful events, try to consider the stressful situation in a broader context and keep a long-term perspective. Avoid blowing the event out of proportion.

9. Maintaining a hopeful outlook. An optimistic outlook enables you to expect that good things will happen in your life. Try visualising what you want, rather than worrying about what you fear.

10. Taking care of yourself. Pay attention to your own needs and feelings. Engage in activities that you enjoy and find relaxing. Exercise regularly. Taking care of yourself helps to keep your mind and body primed to deal with situations that require resilience.

The key is to identify ways that are likely to work well for you as part of your own personal strategy for fostering resilience.

In their groundbreaking book, *The Power of Full Engagement,* Jim Loehr and Tony Schwartz suggest getting more done (with higher levels of satisfaction) is not about managing time, it's about managing your four sources of energy: physical, emotional, mental and spiritual. With each source, we must find a way to balance energy use and energy renewal. When any energy source is out of balance we become burned out and our performance suffers.

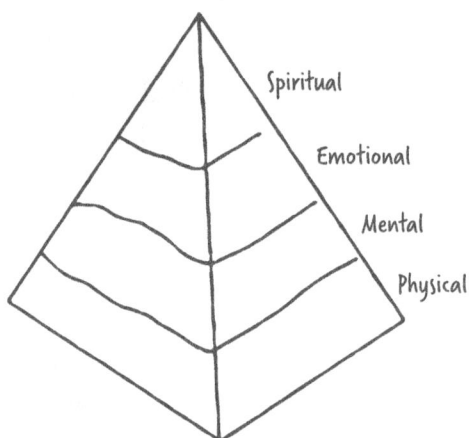

Figure 17: The four sources energy (Jim Loehr and Tony Schwartz)

To change this, we must increase the capacity of each energy source by pushing beyond our normal limits, then renew the source with a corresponding rest period. It's exactly the way we increase our physical strength; we work a muscle to exhaustion, then we rest it. The exertion and rest period makes the muscle stronger. We need to be able to balance the degree of work and rest—but too much rest means the muscle will atrophy.

In our increasingly-busy lives, finding—or more accurately, creating—periods of rest or 'down time' seems difficult. Just as cleaning our teeth is a ritual developed over time, we equally need to create positive energy rituals in our lives. Rituals are specific routines that we do without even thinking about them.

The number of hours in a day is fixed, but the quantity and quality of energy available to us is not. This fundamental insight has the power to revolutionise the way we live. In order to build resilience and develop our capability to not just 'cope' with what life throws at us, we need to do four things:

- *Mobilise* four key sources of energy.
- *Balance* energy expenditure with intermittent energy renewal.
- *Expand* capacity in the same systematic way that elite athletes do.
- *Create* highly specific, positive energy management rituals.

After a fairly lengthy conversation which touched a number of areas, Robert could see a glimmer of hope. He could see that he was not a victim of circumstance and could actually change his life for the better. He could see that his choices and way of seeing things had created the world he now called his life.

Building your 'resilient muscle' is an individual experience. Adapt these tips for your own situation, keeping in mind what has and has not worked for you in the past.

Robert engaged those around him to get involved, and also for support. Many of us feel exactly the same way Robert did, but instead of sharing it, we choose to keep it to ourselves because that's what everyone else does.

Focusing more on enhancing our physical, emotional, mental and spiritual (purpose and meaning) capabilities will pay huge dividends. It'll enable you to develop a reservoir of internal resources that you can draw upon, allowing you to not just cope with life, but thrive and prosper. Applying the principles of positive psychology and strengths-based leadership can also make a big difference. Anything else is selling yourself, and those who care about you, short. And frankly, you're worth it.

Summary

Leadership can take a large toll on people, sometimes robbing them of their sense of enjoyment and fulfilment for their work. This can also impact sleep, health and overall wellbeing.

Resilience is the process of adapting well in the face of adversity, trauma, tragedy, threats, or even significant sources of stress – such as family and relationship problems, serious health problems, or workplace and financial stressors.

Resilience is not a trait that people either have or do not have. It involves behaviours, thoughts, and actions that can be learned and developed in anyone.

A combination of factors contributes to resilience:

- Caring and supportive relationships.
- The capacity to make realistic plans and take steps to carry them out.
- A positive view of yourself, and confidence in your strengths and abilities.
- Skills in communication and problem-solving.
- The capacity to manage strong feelings and impulses.

Engagement and resilience is not about managing time, it's about managing the four sources of energy: physical, emotional, mental and spiritual. With each source, we must find a way to balance energy use and energy renewal. When any energy source is out of balance we become burned out and our performance suffers.

CHAPTER 18

YOU

Robert was struggling to communicate a vision or strategy for API. We have already discussed his lack of authenticity and failure to connect with people in a meaningful way, or influence them effectively. If Robert and his executive team weren't really connected to the mission, vision and values, how could they expect others to be?

Leadership comes from a deeper reality; it comes from our values, principles, life experiences and essence. It is a whole-of-person action. Character is the essence of a leader and works to transform and open up possibilities and potential.

Robert and many members of his team came from a pattern of coping, where they tended to react to circumstances to elicit an immediate result. Coping leaders are often defensive, controlling, aggressive, have a 'win-lose' mentality and resist change. Many of these negative attributes are driven by self-limiting beliefs. 'If I don't act in an authoritative way, people won't do what they're supposed to', or 'I have to know the answer to appear credible', or 'I like to challenge and show the holes in people's arguments.' The exploration of beliefs and taking people through a process to deepen each person's understanding of their world view is often transformational.

Robert and the team eventually engaged some outside support to develop their leadership capability in the area of character and mastery. Some of the things they worked on were:

- Learning to take full responsibility for outcomes.

- Raising awareness of their individual and collective beliefs, and working through the limiting beliefs.

- Developing strategies to lead and live through their character (rather than coping mechanisms).

- Learning how to support each other, including 'calling' behaviours, which were dysfunctional.

- Gaining a sense of purposefulness, both individually and as a team.

After several months of working on themselves, there was a renewed sense of energy and clarity around the mission, vision and values. They had learned how to have robust, crucial conversations. Levels of trust had improved, although actions speak louder than words, so this will take more time. Relationships within the team had improved markedly, and progress had been made outside the team. There was a sense of purpose that was being felt right throughout API. They had learned how to tell a *turnaround story* that engaged and energised the workforce.

Robert and the team had learned some key principles around adaptive leadership and were starting to empower individuals, teams and business units to make progress on their toughest challenges. Change was being managed and led in a systemic and thoughtful way. This had freed up the executive team to focus on strategic leadership and remove the organisation-wide impediments to progress.

Robert also noticed that his energy had returned and he was feeling optimistic about the future. He noticed that relationships at work felt much easier, and even enjoyable again. Importantly, API started to show substantial improvements in innovation and collaboration, and performance was improving. The organisation had stopped haemorrhaging and was on the road to recovery.

Summary

Leadership comes from a deeper reality; it comes from our values, principles, life experiences and essence. It is a whole-of-person action. Character is the essence of a leader and works to transform and open up possibilities and potential.

This is the converse of coping, where leaders are defensive, controlling, aggressive, have a 'win-lose' mentality and resist change. Many of these negative attributes are driven by self-limiting beliefs.

Managers need to develop their leadership capability in the areas of character and mastery. More specifically:

- Learning to take full responsibility for outcomes.
- Raising awareness of their individual and collective beliefs and working through the limiting beliefs.
- Developing strategies to lead and live through their character (rather than coping mechanisms).
- Learning how to support each other, including 'calling' behaviours, which are dysfunctional.
- Gaining a sense of purposefulness, both individually and as a team.

CHAPTER 19

FINAL THOUGHTS: WHAT TO DO WITH THIS LEADERSHIP DECLARATION

The aim of writing this book—particularly our Leadership Declaration—is to inspire and ignite leadership action that makes a difference for you, your organisation and the world you live in.

Its purpose is to clearly state the case for leadership and its importance to all of us at this time. At an organisational level, there is little doubt that real leadership is the 'engine room' of performance. In the absence of systemic, results-focused leadership, breakthrough performance and high commitment will not be achieved.

To make progress on our most significant issues, I believe that we need a new paradigm of leadership that supersedes the outdated industrial age leadership paradigm and liberates us from old ways of thinking about how to manage and lead people. A new paradigm needs to guide our actions and decisions in a constructive, values-driven way. It is one that will empower each of us to take full responsibility and accountability at all levels of organisations, in government, and in the community. Importantly, a new paradigm will create an environment of high levels of commitment and learning.

We have discussed a number of important challenges centred around the idea of leadership and what it means in an organisational context. The very use of the word 'leader' is flawed, because it is usually associated with a position or title, rather than an action. This misconception is shaped throughout our life, helping to create the 'Age of Passivity', which can best be described as learning to rely too heavily on those who hold authority to show us the way. Leadership should be encouraged 'top to bottom' in organisations, regardless of the amount of authority vested in any one individual. Those who choose leadership can enhance their effectiveness significantly by understanding the dynamics and differences between technical and adaptive elements of the challenge.

Despite many theories and countless books about leadership that have sought to enhance our understanding, it is my belief that there are no easy answers or 'silver bullets'. The exercise of leadership is a delicate, yet deliberate blend of character, connection, courage and capability.

A new paradigm creates enormous possibility for organisations and the societies in which we live. The limits to human potential and ingenuity have barely been tested. A new paradigm holds the promise of at least elevating our chances of creating more humanistic, inspiring places for people to innovate and produce products and services that will create breakthrough performance and make a difference.

We are interested in developing leaders from many different industries, fields and walks of life. We have had the privilege over many years to come into contact with some wonderful leaders – the men and women who are able to continually meet or exceed performance expectations, while having the wonderful ability to draw forth the great potential of those around them.

If you find the ideas in this book enticing, or you find that you are already aligned to a new leadership paradigm as discussed, here's what you can do:

- Generate a conversation with your colleagues about the ideas in this book and see what they think.

- Send us an email with your thoughts on Leadership Without Silver Bullets.

- Invite people to a brown paper bag lunch meeting where you will discuss this book and the new leadership paradigm.

- Take a stand for leadership and leadership development in your organisation. If you need support in bringing a leadership development focus to your organisation, please call us for a free consultation.

If you would like more information on how The Leadership Sphere can help you improve the leadership capability in your organisation to deliver breakthrough performance, please contact:

phillipr@theleadershipsphere.com.au

www.theleadershipsphere.com.au

Order copies at: www.theleadershipsphere.com.au

ABOUT THE AUTHOR

I became interested in leadership when I joined the Victoria Police Psychology Unit in the early 80s. I had a broad role supporting people across the spectrum from dysfunctionality through to elite squads.

Later, I received approval to work with 500 operational police, over a year, to shift their health, wellbeing and productivity (which was also the subject of my Master's thesis). The task was to influence busy operational police to move away from unhealthy and potentially damaging health behaviours towards healthy living. The results after one year demonstrated substantial positive change and health outcomes, putting the equivalent of fifty police officers back on the street due to a reduction in sick leave, injuries and other poor outcomes. The program ran successfully for the next two decades.

I was also lucky enough to help design and deliver a five-day training program (Project Beacon) to 10,000 operational police to improve the poor track record of police shootings—one of the highest in the world at the time. The program aimed to change the culture and approach to critical incidents where suspects may be armed, drug or alcohol affected and/or suffering from some type of psychiatric episode. The focus was on improved planning and communication skills, and achieved significant reductions in fatal shootings.

After 17 years in Victoria Police, and having 'cut my teeth' as an operational police officer, trainer, facilitator and coach, it was time for a bigger challenge.

In 2001, I worked at the ANZ Bank in the Breakout and Cultural Transformation Program where I was the Head of Consulting and Program Delivery, responsible for delivery of individual and team development programs to 40,000 people across many countries over six years. Breakout has been widely acclaimed as one of the best examples of a successful cultural transformation program in the world.

I founded and launched The Leadership Sphere in 2007, where my colleagues and I consult to some of the largest companies in the world in the areas of leadership development, team development and culture change.

I live in the beautiful city of Melbourne with my wife, Kerrie and three children (21, 21, and 17 years old). My hobbies include keeping fit by jogging and cycling, vicariously participating in many sports, reading, aviation and dining.

CONTACT/ORGANISATION DETAILS

The Leadership Sphere was formed in 2007 by Phillip Ralph and Associates, who have a long history of creating high-performing, humanistic and healthy workplaces through effective leadership and teams. We do this through the design and delivery of evidence-based, world-class solutions such as workshop facilitation, coaching and consulting.

The Leadership Sphere (TLS) partners with organisations to achieve sustainable high performance through a powerful multi-disciplinary approach, focusing in the areas of leadership development, team development and cultural transformation. Our point of difference is a structured systemic approach to achieve realistic and sustainable positive change, leading to breakthrough performance.

Our prestigious clients include a wide range of major companies across the public sector and private industry, many of whom are Top 100 ASX companies. We have services in all states of Australia and in the United States, the United Kingdom, New Zealand, Hong Kong, Singapore, Spain and the Netherlands.

Why do we do what we do?

We do what we do for one simple, yet compelling reason: to see every individual, team and organisation unlock the potential and energy that will make all the difference.

Who do we work with?

- Managing Directors and CEOs.
- Senior executives.

- Leaders.
- High potential/fast track employees.
- Leaders in transition.
- Organisations that want high-performance cultures (including increasing engagement).
- Teams that have a desire to excel.

We work with senior leaders and teams at the intrapersonal, interpersonal and group levels. By working at multiple levels, we are able to help our clients achieve significant shifts that stick.

We are renowned in the marketplace for the following:

1. Making the desired happen (individual, team and organisational transformation).
2. Our transparent business model, which indicates a clear scope of work and costs.
3. We deliver what we say we're going to deliver.

Our Values

Our values are important to us. These are the non-negotiable minimum standards to which all our work and dealings apply. These values are not a high aspiration we strive for, but rather the way we do business. When we are true to our values, our clients know it.

Customer

Being the best for our clients means a customer-driven approach rather than a provider- or product-driven approach. This may seem pedantic, but it makes all the difference. Many consultants and coaches start with their paradigm or framework and fit that to their clients, rather than other way around. At TLS, we work back from the client's needs and customise the approach to optimise outcomes.

Partnership

We adopt a partnering approach for several reasons. First, we prefer that our clients have energy and buy-in around the reasons we were hired in the first place. The desired change will simply not be self-sustaining otherwise. Second, we consciously work to transfer skill and knowledge where applicable. This helps ensure a system which is self-reinforcing and sustaining. Third, it is more enjoyable for both us and the clients when we work together to solve problems.

Ethical Practice

Ethical practice means never compromising our own integrity or that of our clients. Again, many consultants and coaches collude with the client system by 'selling in' products and services that don't address the true underlying issues. While we can provide you or your people with off-the-shelf products, we will always alert you to the pros and cons. Practising in an ethical manner means that we work in the best interests of our clients, not us.

Leadership

Leadership to us means being at the forefront of the latest thinking from around the world so we can bring the best to our clients. It is also reflected in how we engage with all our stakeholders, be they clients, suppliers, government or our own people. We believe that we can make a powerful difference in the world, both through leaders and by being leaders. Making a difference means enabling people to be all they can be, regardless of the organisation, culture, gender, race or age. The bottom line is people living more fulfilling lives in a sustainable way.

Courage

Being courageous comes in many forms. For us, however, it means being bold and different as consultants. It means doing things differently from the pack – creating value beyond the norm by putting ourselves out there. Our consultants and coaches need to demonstrate and model the behaviours that we ask of our clients, whether they are a senior leader or a team that feels stuck. We need to be prepared to go to the hard places to help our clients.

Excellence

It means striving to be the best in whatever we do, not so we can say we're the best compared to others, but so we can say we were the best for our client. It also means having the best people working for us. Our clients rightly expect work of the highest quality – accurate, valuable, on time, on budget and with no surprises.

Community

We have a strong sense of doing what is right for the community and feel a responsibility to all people. We have a desire for a world that is peaceful, equitable and where people are honest with one another. We value spouses, children and family. We want everyone to have the opportunity to grow and be the best they can be, whatever this means for them.

The Leadership Sphere Pty Ltd
Level 2, GPO Building
350 Bourke Street
Melbourne, Victoria 3000
info@theleadershipsphere.com.au
www.theleadershipsphere.com.au
www.phillipralph.com

If you would like to purchase additional copies or any of our other books, please visit www.theleadershipsphere.com.au.

REFERENCES

Anon., n.d. *VIA Institute on Character.* [Online] Available at: http://www.viacharacter.org/www/Character-Strengths-Survey

Beer, M., 2009. *High Commitment High Performance: How to Build a Resilient Organization for Sustained Advantage.* s.l.: San Francisco: Jossey-Bass.

Boston, W. & Wilkes, W., 2016. *New York Times.* [Online] Available at: http://www.wsj.com/articles/former-volkswagen-ceo-martin-winterkorn-faces-market-manipulation-probe-in-germany-1466432926

Burns, J. M., 1978. *Leadership.* New York: Harper Perennial Modern Classics.

Cashman, K., 2008. *Leadership from the Inside Out: Becoming a leader for life.* 2nd ed. San Francisco: Berrett-Koehler Publishers Inc.

Center For Climate Change Energy Solutions, 2015. *Outcomes of the U.N. Climate Change Conference in Paris.* [Online] Available at: http://www.c2es.org/international/negotiations/cop21-paris/summary

Changing Minds, 2009. *Leadership Theories.* [Online] Available at: http://changingminds.org/disciplines/leadership/theories/leadership_theories.htm [Accessed May 2017].

Clance, P. R. & James, S. A., 1978. The Imposter Phenomemon in High Performing Women: dynamics and theraputic intervention. *Psycotherapy: Theory, Research and Practice,* Volume 15 (3), p. 241–247. Georgia State University, University Plaza, Atlanta, Georgia 30303.

Covey, S (2006), *The Speed of Trust: The One Think that Changes*, Simon and Schuster, Australia.

Deutschman, A., 2007. Change or Die: The Three Keys to Change at Work and in Life. *Fast Company*, 02 January. Atlanta, Georgia.

Dobbs, R., Manyika, J. & Woetzel, J., 2015. *The Four Global Forces Breaking all the Trends.* s.l.: London, San Francisco & Shanghai: McKinsey Global Institute.

Drinon, R., n.d. *Refining Your Leadership Philosophy and Style.* s.l.:s.n. North America.

Duhigg, C., 2016. *What Google Learned From Its Quest to Build the Perfect Team.* [Online]
Available at: http://www.nytimes.com/2016/02/28/magazine/what-google-learned-from-its-quest-to-build-the-perfect-team.html
[Accessed May 2017].

Dweck, C. S., 2006. *Mindset: The New Psychology of Success.* NY: Random House Publishing Group.

Edelman, R., 2009. *Edelman Trust Barometer Executive Summary,* New York: Richard Edelman.

Gardner, J. W., 1965. How to Prevent Organizational Dry Rot. *Harper's Magazine,* October.pp. pp. 20-26. Rice University (Texas).

Gerzon, M., 2003. Leaders and Leadership. *Beyond Intractability,* September. University of Colorado, Boulder.

Geus, A. d., 1988. Planning as Learning. *Harvard Business Review,* March-April 1988 pp. 70-74.

Handy, C., 2006. Philosopher Leaders. In: *The Leader of the Future: Visions, Strategies, and Practices for the New Era.* San Francisco: Jossey-Bass.

Heifetz, R., 1999. *Leadership vs Authority.* s.l.:s.n.

Heifetz, R. A., Grashow, A. & Linsky, M., 2009. *The Practice of Adaptive Leadership: Tools and Tactics for Challenging Your Organisation and the World.* s.l.:Harvard Business Press.

Heifetz, R. A., Linsky, M. & Grashow, A., 2009. *The Practice of Adaptive Leadership: Tools and Tactics for Changing Your Organisation and the World.* Boston, Massachusetts: Harvard Business Press.

Heifetz, R. & Laurie, D. L., 2001. The Work of Leadership. *Harvard Business Review,* December.

Hock, D., 1999. *Birth of the Charodic Age.* San Francisco: Berrett-Koelher.

Hollander, E. P., 1978. *Leadership Dynamics: A Practical Guide to Effective Relationships.* New York: Free Press.

Linksy, M. & Heifetz, R. A., 2002. *Leadership on the Line: Staying Alive through the Dangers of Leading.* Boston: Harvard Business School Press.

Maister, D., Green, C. & Galford, R., 2001. *The Trusted Advisor.* s.l.:Touchstone.

Margaret Thatcher Foundation, 1981. *The Art and Science of Leadership,* s.l.: s.n.

McGrath, M., 2016. *How The Wells Fargo Phony Account Scandal Sunk John Stimpf.* [Online]
Available at: http://www.forbes.com/sites/
maggiemcgrath/2016/09/23/the-9-most-important-things-you-need-to-know-about-the-well-fargo-fiasco/#22e9c5437dcb

Pink, D., 2013. *To Sell is Human: The Surprising truth About Moving Others.* s.l.: USA: Riverhead Books.

Prince, C., Picknett, L., Prior, S. & Brydon, R., 2002. *War of the Windsors: A Century of Unconstitutional Monarchy.* s.l.: Edinburgh, UK: Mainstream Publishing.

Rost, J., 1993. *Leadership for the 21st Century.* Westport: Praeger Publishers.

Rost, J., 1997. Moving from Indivdual to Relationship: A Postindustrial Paradigm of Leadership. *Journal of Leadership Studies,* 4(4), p. 3–16. Toronto, Ontario.

Schein, E., 2006. Leadership Competencies: A Provocative New Look. In: *The Leader of the Future: Visions, Strategies, and Practices for the New Era.* San Francisco: Jossey-Bass.

Sinek, S., 2011. *Start with why: How great leaders inspire everyone to take action.* s.l.: New York: Portfolio.

Smith, G., 2016. *Deutsche Bank Wants Bonus Millions Back From It's Former CEOs.* [Online]
Available at: http://fortune.com/2016/11/17/deutsche-bank-clawback-ceo-bonuses/

Williams, D., 2005. *Real Leadership: Helping People and Organisations Face Their Toughest Challenges.* San Francisco: Berret-Koehler Publishers.

World Bank, 2016. *Poverty and Shared Prosperity 2016: Taking on Equality,* Washington: International Bank for Reconstruction and Development/ The World Bank.

Wortmann, C., 2006. *What's Your Story?.* Chicago: Kaplan Publishing.

BIBLIOGRAPHY

Buckingham, M (2007). *Go Put Your Strengths to Work: 6 Powerful Steps to Achieve Outstanding Performance.* New York: One Thing Productions.

Brookfields, SD (1991). *Developing Critical Thinkers.* Oxford: Jossey-Bass Publishers.

Cashman, K (2003). *Awakening the Leader Within: A Story of Transformation.* New Jersey: John Wiley & Sons, Inc.

Camillus, JC (2008). "Strategy as a Wicked Problem", *Harvard Business Review.*

Covey, S (2004). *The 8th Habit: From Effectiveness to Greatness* New York: Free Press.

Crum, TF, & Denver J (1987). *The Magic of Conflict: Turning Life of Work into a Work of Art.* New York: Rockefeller Centre.

Csikszentmihalyi, M (2000). "The Contribution of Flow to Positive Psychology" *in The Science of Optimism and Hope.* Ed. J.E. Gillham, 387-Radnor, PA: Templeton Foundation Press.

Gallwey, WT (2003). *The Inner Game of Work: Overcoming Mental Obstacles for Maximum Performance.* London: Random House.

Gardner, H (2004). *Changing Minds.* Boston: Harvard Business School Press.

Gladwell, M (2005). *Blink.* Sydney: Allen Lane (Penguin Group).

Goleman, D (2006). *Social Intelligence – The New Science of Human Relationships.* London: Hutchinson.

Goleman D (2003). *Destructive Emotions and How We Can Overcome Them.* Great Britain: Batman Books.

Gahan, P., Adamovic, M., Bevitt, A., Harley, B., Healy, J., Olsen, J.E., Theilacker, M. 2016. Leadership at Work: Do Australian leaders have what it takes? Melbourne: Centre for Workplace Leadership, University of Melbourne. Available at: workplaceleadership.com.au/sal

Greenleaf, RK (1991). *Servant Leadership*. New York: Paulist Press, New York.

Heifetz, RA, & Linsky, M (2002). "A survival guide for leaders", *Harvard Business Review*.

Heifetz, RA, & Laurie, DL (2002). "The Work of Leadership", *Harvard Business Review*.

Goleman, D (1998). "What Makes a Leader?", *Harvard Business Review*.

Kegan R, & Lahey LL (2009). *Immunity to Change: How to Overcome it and Unlock the Potential in Yourself and Your Organization*. Boston: Harvard Business School.

Keith, K (2006). *Engagement is Not Enough: You Need Passionate Employees to Achieve Your Dream*. San Diego: Advantage Publishing.

Kouzes, J (2003). *Business Leadership*. San Francisco: Jossey-Bass.

Lee, G (2003). *Leadership Coaching*. London: CIPD (Chartered Institute of Personnel Development).

Levitt, SD & Dubner, SJ (2005). *Freakonomics*. Melbourne: Penguin Books Ltd.

Linley, AP & Joseph, S (Ed.) (2004). *Positive Psychology in Practice*. New Jersey: John Wiley and Sons.

Maister, DH Green, CH, Galford, R.M. (2000). *The Trusted Advisor*. New York: Free Press.

Malandro, L (2003). *Say it Right, The First Time*. New York: McGraw-Hill.

Martin, R (2007). "Choices, Conflict, and the Creative Spark. The Problem- Solving Power of Integrative Thinking", Excerpted from *The Opposable Mind: How Successful Leaders Win Through Integrative Thinking*, Harvard Business Press.

Parashar, F (2003). *The Balancing Act: Work-Life Solutions for Busy People*. Sydney: Simon & Schuster.

Patterson, K., Grenny, J., McMillan, R., Switzler A., (2002). *Crucial Conversations: Tools for Talking Tough When Stakes are High.* New York: McGraw-Hill.

Pink, D (2006). *A Whole New Mind: Why Right-Brainers Will Rule the Future.* Riverhead Trade.

Seligman, EP (2004). *Character Strengths and Virtues: A Handbook and Classification.* Oxford University Press.

Ray, M (2005). *The Highest Goal: The Secret That Sustains You In Every Moment.* San Francisco: Berrett-Koehler.

Pfeffer, J (1998). *Human Equation: Building Profits by Putting People First.* Boston: Harvard Business School Press.

Scott, S (2002). *Fierce Conversations: Achieving Success in Work and in Life, One Conversation at a Time.* London: Judy Piatkus (Publishers) Limited.

Seligman, EP (2002). *Authentic Happiness – Using the New Positive Psychology to Realize Your Potential for Lasting Fulfillment.* Random House: Sydney.

Senge, P, Sharmer, CO, Jaworski, J, Flowers, BS (2004). *Presence: Human Purpose and the Field of the Future.* Massachusetts: The Society for Organizational Learning.

Snyder, CR, & Lopez, SJ (2007). *Positive Psychology – The Scientific and Practical Explorations of Human Strengths.* London: Sage Publications.

Stober, DR, & Grant AM (Eds) (2006). *Evidence Based Coaching Handbook.* United States: John Wiley & Sons.

Wageman, R, Nunes, DA, Burruss, JA, Hackman, JR (2008). *Senior Leadership Teams: What it Takes to Make them Great.* Boston: Harvard Business School Publishing.

Whitmore J (2002). *Coaching for Performance: Growing People, Performance and Purpose.* London: WS Bookwell.

ON-LINE RESOURCES

The Leadership Sphere
www.theleadershipsphere.com.au

Phillip Ralph
www.phillipralph.com

Actionable Conversations (TLS is an accredited partner)
www.actionable.co

Experience Point (with IDEO) – Change and Innovation Business
Simulations (TLS is an accredited partner)
www.experiencepoint.com

TakeON! (TLS is an accredited partner)
www.takeon.biz

Harvard Business Review
www.hbr.org

McKinsey Quarterly
www.mckinseyquarterly.com

Managerial Executive Wellbeing Survey (MEWS) at
www.theleadershipsphere.com.au

Ted – a not-for-profit site dedicated to Ideas Worth Spreading
www.ted.com

University of Pennsylvania - Authentic Happiness
www.authentichappiness.sas.upenn.edu

University of Pennsylvania - Positive Psychology Centre
www.ppc.sas.upenn.edu

www.ingramcontent.com/pod-product-compliance
Lightning Source LLC
Chambersburg PA
CBHW071552200326

41519CB00021BB/6707